MY POETRY DEPICTS YOU

An anthology of contemporary Kurdish poetry

Dr Rebwar Fatah

To Laylan, Sheelan and Chnoor

Name of the book: My poetry depicts you
An anthology of contemporary Kurdish poetry
Author: Dr Rebwar Fatah
All photographs are taken by meriwani art

Publisher: meriwani art
First Edition London 2017
Second Edition London 2017
Edition 2.a London April 2018
Third Edition London May 2019
Selection copyright © Dr Rebwar Fatah 2019
ASIN: 1976719127

Table of Contents

Introduction

I have been translating Kurdish poetry into English for over three decades now. The intention of publishing these poems as a collection arose few years ago. The translation of each poem resulted out of a spontaneous mood, yet intentional drive on various occasions. I translated some poems following requests made by friends and others out of a personal passion to escape the pressures of work and life.

As I was assembling the collection, I realised that it could be of real interest to poetry aficionados and readers of Kurdish and Middle Eastern literature. The anthology is rare in the sense that there have not been many similar attempts before.

Poetry has never been alien to me. I was raised in a family that brought forth two known poets, my older brothers: late Dilshad Meriwani (1947-1989) and Goran Meriwani (1955-present). At home, I was surrounded by a library of literary and poetic value. As a young man, I used to write poetry myself, some of which was featured in prominent Iraqi Kurdish publications. On one occasion, one of my Kurdish poems was translated into Arabic and published in a newspaper in Baghdad.

This anthology is a general introduction to contemporary Kurdish poetry, which may not be familiar to English speaking readers.

These poems are from different time periods and were written under various oppressive Iraqi regimes. Most of the poets included in this anthology were active during the former ruling Baath Party. Unfortunately, three of the writers, Dilshad Meriwani, Mala Ali and Barzan Osman, were executed under the Baath regime. Two others were also killed. Bakir Ali was allegedly murdered by Kurdish security services while leading a peaceful protest. Irfan Ahmed died under suspicious circumstances whilst in Kurdish detention. All the other poets, with the exception of three, fled in the hope for international protection as a consequence of their activities. Some were reunited with their homeland after the Kurdistan Regional Government had been established in the early 1990s.

The state of exile enriched Kurdish literature. Due to the work of these excommunicated authors, a new branch of Kurdish literature emerged, which can be regarded as Kurdish Diaspora literature. This new wave of poetry in Kurdistan had been influenced by Western literature. Living under oppression proved to be integral to the work of Kurdish poets. Their stories are weaved into their poetry. Short biographies of each poet are provided in this anthology to contextualise the author and his work.

Contemporary Kurdish Poetry

This anthology comprises two different types of poetry, the first being a less traditional form and the second, called *Robayyat*, stems from the Kurdistan region of Iraq. *Robayyat* is usually expressed through quatrains, i.e. four-liners, the verse rhyming AABA. The majority of the poems were written after the turn of the twentieth century and the establishment of what is now known as the "Contemporary Kurdish School of Poetry", or the "Goran School of Poetry".

The predominant pioneers of this school were Sheikh Nuri Sheikh Salih (1868 - 1958), Rashid Najib (1906 – 1968), Rafiq Hilmi (1898 - 1960), Abdulrahman Bagi Baban - also known as Abdulrahamn Bagi Nifus (1878-1967) and Abdullah Goran (1904 -

1962). Sheik Salih, who is regarded as the theoretician behind this school, was influenced by Turkish contemporary poetry at the time. After his continuous studies of poetry, Sheikh Salih concluded that some traditional principles should be maintained in the creation of contemporary poetry. Most sources believe that Sheikh Salih was the mastermind who started the new school that originated between 1920 and 1930. Hilmi states that Sheikh Salih laid the foundation stones for contemporary Kurdish poetry with the rest of writers following his example.

In one of Sheikh Salih's articles (1926), he identifies three principals for poetry: rhythm, rhyme and idea. However, there is another poet of equal innovative worth who must not be forgotten. In an interview published in 1971, Goran stated that Baban wrote contemporary poetry before Sheikh Salih, but his poetry remained unpublished at the time and merely within the grasp of a closed circle of people. A small collection of Baban's poetry was published in 1989, even though he started writing poetry in 1913. Unfortunately, most of his poems composed between 1913 and 1919 were lost.

The contemporary school cannot be linked to merely one individual, but to several progressive minds who all stemmed from the small city of Sulaymaniyah. These intellectuals were close friends linked through bloodlines. It is fair to state that the contemporary school resulted out of the poets' joint efforts, the increasing social awareness and the rising of Kurdish patriotism in the early 20th century.

Goran has to be acknowledged as another pioneering mind because he developed a different style after 1930. The reasons for Goran's individuality amongst his peers are manifold. While most of them were active in the early days of establishing the poetry school, they slowed down for different reasons, one of them being their demanding roles as civil servants. This was definitely the case for Rashid Najib who was a high-ranking civil servant. Two of Goran's collections of poetry were published in 1950 while Sheikh Salih's collection was first published 20 years later, in 1970, and by then people were more familiar with Goran than Sheikh Salih.[1] Baban's first collection was only published in 1989. With the foundation of contemporary poetry already established and readers recovered from the psychological threshold of modernisation, Goran's mind was forward-facing and analytical. He worked on other aspects of modernisation such as the subject and its unity, the vocabulary and poetic meters. In fact, some of Goran's poems can be confused for folksongs. This made Goran's poetry more accessible to the wider population and even replaced some of the folk lyrics in popular songs; whilst other poets never reached the ear of the masses. Unlike others, Goran was an active writer. He published the majority of his poems as he wrote them. This preserved his work as it was released immediately to the readers. He had been officially established as a contemporary poet.

Goran, in addition to his work as a writer, was a politician associated with an extremely popular communist party at the time. As a member, he was sent to represent the party in several international conferences. This introduced him to communities outside Kurdistan, in particular Iraq and the wider international community. His association with Radio Haifa, a broadcast in Kurdish, also helped him to spread his net across a wider Kurdish population.

Another pivotal poet of the 20th century is Tawfeq Mahmoud Hamza, also known as Piramerd (1867 – 1950). Although his name is not usually linked to the school, it is difficult to imagine contemporary Kurdish poetry without Piramerd. He is not included

---

[1] Only a modest collection of around 40 pages of poetry written by Sheikh Salih was published in 1958 in Sulaymaniyah.

in this collection because he requires a special focus as he is essential to the contemporary Kurdish intellectual life. In addition to being a poet and a great thinker, he was a journalist who modernised Kurdish literature. To some extent, Piramerd was a leading social and literary figure in the first part of the 20ᵗʰ century. For example, Newroz ceremonies, as we know them today in the Kurdistan region of Iraq, were initiated by Piramerd. "Newroz" is the celebration of the New Year, which is the first day of spring, March 21ˢᵗ, and is celebrated by many people around the world.

The Kurds were joined by neighbouring people as they embarked on the path of contemporary poetry. Around the same period, Ottoman poets who were part of the literary community joined the cause: Fajri Ati (Fecri Ati) (1909 – 1912), Tofiq Fikret (1867 –1915), Namık Kemal (1840 –1888), Abdulhak Hamid Tarhan (1852 – 1937) and Jalal Sahir (1883 - 1935). The Arab Iraqi poets, Badr Shakir al-Sayyab (1926 – 1964) and Nazik al-Malaika (1923 – 2007), and Iran's Nima Yushij (1895 –1960) were involved in the contemporary poetry movement.

Kurdish poetry had been modernised by these exemplary pioneers as their style differentiated itself from the classical poets before them. However, they did not exclude classical traits in their writings. Not only did the poetry change, but the target readers evolved too. Prior to these social alterations, the intellectual elite were the only ones who could understand Kurdish poetry, mostly because of its heavy use of classical Arabic and Farsi vocabulary. In addition, its rhythm was complicated, conforming to the Arabic *Arud or* "science of poetry" established in the eighth century, and imposed a certain linguistic structure that made it almost incomprehensible to the common ear. In fact, the language found in classical poetry appeared to be Kurdish rather than actually being Kurdish. Poetry was reserved for a privileged class and recited aloud in a Diwakhan – a guest room where only men gathered for fun and poetry readings. Additionally, poetry was the conversational topic in mosques where religiously educated people studied and led discussions as poetry was sung during religious ceremonies and rituals. Poets like Bekhud (1879 – 1955) and Mahwi (1836-1906) wrote mostly spiritual poems with extremely difficult vocabulary. Within this context, poetry was out of reach for ordinary people.

The rhymed classic Kurdish poetry possesses different "meters"; that are known in Arabic as "seas" or buh'ur (singular bah'r). The measuring unit of "seas" is known as "taf'ylah", and every "sea" contains a certain number of tafylas, that construct the verse or bayt of the poem. Every bayt ends with the same rhyme or qaflyah throughout the poem.

The modernisation of Kurdish poetry did not just undergo one change, but almost all aspects were altered. For example, there were significant linguistic changes and poetic topics varied across all aspects of life. Ultimately, rhyme and rhythm moved away from the traits of Arabic Aruz classical poetry.

The poets of the mid-last century simplified the vocabulary by uniting it with the common spoken language. Their rhythms were based on popular Kurdish folk songs. This is called "ke'shi birgayy" or syllabus-based meter, also known as "keshi panja" or "haja". This meter had been used before the Arabic Arud meters infiltrated Kurdish poetry. For example, Mawlawi (1806 – 1882) and Besarani (1643 – 1702) wrote all their poetry in the Gorani dialect in a 10 syllabus-meter. They used a set of two rhyming couplets known as the AABB, two rhyming lines of the same length.

The audience of poetry also changed. Poetry no longer reflected only a privileged few, but a diverse community of voices. Poetry was now taught at emerging public schools at the time and had distanced itself from the exclusive circles of religious and intellectual elites. The seed for change in the educational system had been planted.

Contemporary Kurdish poetry was not only wearing a new cover, rhyme and rhythms, but the subjects evolved alongside everything else. Poems were now addressing the problems of ordinary people and were not only songs anymore that were dedicated to God, the prophet or love affairs of privileged classes.

Contributors

Sadly, as with many cultures throughout history, the arena of Kurdish literature was dominated by men. However, I have included two Kurdish female poets in the collection. Venus Faiq and Dilsoz Hama are two female modern writers who are included in the anthology. Fortunately, in recent years more women poets have gained the respect of avid readers from all walks of life.

Below you will find a list naming all the poets represented in this anthology, starting with two poems by Nali (1797–1869) and one poem by Kurdi (1809-1850) to provide a flavour of classical Kurdish poetry, which may be unfamiliar to non-native readers. "Hey enemy" – or *Ay raqib*, in Kurdish – may not fit into this anthology, but I included it nevertheless because of its importance, as it is regarded as the Kurdish national anthem. The poets who contributed to this anthology are (in chronological order):

Nali
Kurdi
Abdullah Goran
Ahmed Hardi
Yunis Rauf Dildar
Kamaran Mukri

Abdullah Pashew
Sherko Bekas
Dilshad Meriwani
Rafiq Sabir
Goran Meriwani
Mohammed Omar Osman
Venus Fiaq
Dilsoz Hama
Barzan Osman
Esmayil Mohammed
Hussein Maulud Ahmed, known as Mala Ali
Bakir Ali
Irfan Ahmed

In the last section you will discover a few poems penned by me.
They are inspired by all the aforementioned writers and whilst they
are not all Kurdish poems, they influenced Kurdish poetry. I have
also included a miscellaneous section for poems that I have
translated and did not wish to include in the main body of the
anthology.

This anthology is by no means a definitive list containing every
Kurdish poet, but I assembled an adequate selection of exemplary
voices. I have deliberately included many poets who have not yet
been introduced to the international community. Every poet
selection contained a personal element for me. Some of the poems
have stayed with me since my youth, and some of the poets are or
were close friends or relatives.

As with many Western poets, some Kurdish writers tend to be
rather subtle in conveying their meaning. This might be a
predominant side of poetry, unlike any other branches of literature.
Some poets, like Dilshad Meriwani, write more clearly, and tell
coherent stories. Others, like Dilsoz Hama and Refiq Sabir, may

only hint at the essential through subtle metaphors and similes. Some poems contain ambiguities, which I have respected in the translation.

The exiled poets, such as Abdulla Pashew and Goran Meriwani, internalised the mechanisms of Western literature and are able to express their Kurdish poetry similar to Western patterns. The latter has recently embarked on a new style of poetry which does not share any poetic patterns established in his own homeland or abroad. He deliberately disrupts the rhythm and destroys known poetic meters. It is an influential method that has been copied by other poets. In contrast to Meriwani, Pashew possesses a different style. He writes mostly in short verses ending with a strong punchline.

However, none of the exiled Kurdish poets totally abandoned the topics close to the hearts of Kurdish people. They still addressed issues that Kurdish communities have to face whether they are in the diaspora or in their homeland.

During the rule of the oppressive Iraqi regime, Kurdish poets developed a vocabulary of "self-censorship" which could only be understood by the intellectual elite in order to avoid persecution. This set of symbols and vocabulary is still used by Kurdish poets, despite having more freedom in the Kurdistan region of Iraq or in exile. Naturally, this coded speech makes translations more complicated.

Translating poetry is never an easy task. It is difficult to do justice to the original; some of the texts' original flavour may be lost, no matter what. For example, the original word order and sounds would be lost in translation. Poetry is language engineering. Some words are connected in an unexpected fashion in the context of ordinary prose and other words with similar sounds are used in a verse to give rhythm to the poem. These subtleties are all lost in translation. The cultural gap between the two languages must also be considered, as the translation changes the cultural symbols. For example, the bird *owl* in Kurdish culture is seen as a curse. In English, however, it is a symbol of message delivery. In addition, a poem can consist of several sceneries connected to certain events of life, some of which may be conveyed; others may not. The translator needs to find equivalent sceneries in the translated language. However, in spite of all this, in order to introduce different cultures to each other, translations must persevere their goal to unite us all.

There is a more fundamental issue with translations. Despite languages being a connecting factor, translating from one into the other can be problematic. Word meanings may differ between languages. A word encapsulates the historical culture of a people or community, which can change with time. Even if an equivalent notion can be found between languages, it may not be accurate. Even an object like an *apple* may be the same in both languages, but Kurdish and English *apples* are different. If a specific apple is named in one language, it may not find resonance and compatibility in the other language. The translation of physical and known objects is less complicated than abstract concepts such as theological vocabulary and mythical stories. The faith and religion of people change from one language to another.

Another specific linguistic issue is non-existence of gender in Kurdish language, while it is clear in English. I have identified the gender in the poems with the help of my cultural background.

In spite of these obstacles, I have given my best to remain true to the original text. In some cases, I was forced to modify the poem in order for it to make sense to the English reader. I have not attempted to turn the poems into English poetry. I translated them to safeguard their original soul.

I have introduced punctuation to the poets' work. The old poems that have always been delivered via word of mouth contained no punctuation whatsoever. The same counts for modern poets who hardly use punctuation as well. Lack of punctuation in writing, poetry and prose, is a Middle Eastern problem. Punctuation is not regarded to be necessary.

Poetry in Kurdish Culture

Poetry is a vital part of Kurdish culture and lifestyle because the Kurdish language has only been available in the written form since 1898 which was the publication date of the first Kurdish paper *'Kurdistan'* in Cairo brought forth by the members of the prominent Kurdish clan *Badirkhan*. Reciting poetry was an easy way to broadcast one's thoughts and opinions through word of mouth. Not only did it dominate Kurdish life, it was also the only type of recorded literature that has been transferred from one generation to another.

Oftentimes, folkloric lyrics have their roots in formally documented literature and even though the original wording could be attributed to a known author in the beginning, through the verbal distribution over time, the lyrics would become folklore and the author anonymous.

For lack of publication, the classical Kurdish poets, placed their pen name in the last verse of the poem. If this verse would get lost, the poem would be converted to folk lyrics, due to the lack of the author's name.

Many Kurdish poets deliberately expressed themselves anonymously, to avoid having to face the usual consequences for publicly voicing their opinions, especially when speaking out against oppression or social humiliation for describing their affection for a woman. These types of poetry are diffused into the common folk literature.

Kurdish folklore is rich with lyrics that are either erotic or romantic. These topics continue to be considered a taboo in Kurdish society, but anonymous poems provided a platform free from censorship. However, the folksingers do sing these erotic lyrics.

Certain patterns of producing folkloric literature can be recognised. Oftentimes, the original verse of a folksong was uttered by an anonymous person; then others built on it, based on other verses on the same notion and rhythm. For example, several folk verses that start by telling the lover, "You visit", then are followed by different words in several versions: "You visit the towns"; "You visit the school" or "You visit the market".

I will provide a relevant example below to clarify the concept. These are several verses of a well-known song addressing "your figures", affections exchanged between male and female lovers.

Place on my heart, all your fingers;
Cool me down with your plait.

Place on my heart, your recorder-like fingers;
Do not deprive me of your rosy lips.

Place on my heart, your slim fingers;
Allow me to guard your prominent breast.

Sometimes the original verse may be identified because it has a landmark built into it, such as a historical element that can be older than what is revealed in the other verses.

Folk lyrics cannot be separated from folk songs, which are a means to mark social occasions such as weddings, deaths, births, and of course private gatherings. Most of the singers hired for these occasions were men as the male love dominated the lyrics.

However, there are lyrics that are clearly expressed by women and they have contributed to the wealth of folklore, despite the fact that female narratives had a history of silence and exclusion. There are, of course, verses that are neutral, sharing common elements, making it difficult to tell whether a man or woman wrote them.

Throughout this anthology, explanatory notes in the footers clarify specific Kurdish issues that are mentioned and the role they played. At times, the subject of a poem needed to be properly introduced and contextualised, an example would be that of extrajudicial killings. If the note is given by the poets themselves it will be referenced as such.

First and Second Edition

The first edition of this ethnography was published as an ebook on Amazon in January 2017. All the poems of the first edition are still included but have been modified. I have assembled more poems of some poets, namely Nali, Sherko Bekas, Goran Meriwani and Ismayil Mohammed. Two more sections – "Inspired" and "Miscellaneous" – have been added to this edition.

I have modified almost every poet biography and the introduction is more substantial in this edition.

Generally, this edition is an improvement in many aspects.

Edition 2.a

Two poems have been added: "Bloody flower" by Abdullah Goran and "Next Time" by Goran Meriwani.

Third Edition

I have reviewed and edited the text where necessary. The introduction is modified. Pieces by Kurdi, Abdullah Goran, Mahwi and Goran Meriwani have been added. The biographies are all modified and improved. This edition is more substantial in every sense. All the photographs are added.

Acknowledgement

This project could have not been completed without the help of the people close to me. I would like to thank those who assisted me during this project. Firstly, my family: Chnoor, Sheelan and Laylan, who have supported me and gave me the freedom and time to work on the anthology.

For editing and reviewing, I am grateful to Alison Azhar, who read some of the translated pieces and contributed to their value and richness. She also encouraged me to translate poetry. Sheri Laizer read some of the poems and edited them. Dr Rashid Kardaghi provided many valuable comments and suggestions. I am grateful to all of them.

Most helpful was Sheelan Fatah, who extensively edited the collection and provided important feedback to bring it to its current status. She read every draft I produced. I am very grateful to her.

The second edition was polished with the help of Ruth Embaie, who read the book thoroughly to provide valuable feedback which is reflected in the current edition. I am grateful to her.

For the third edition, I am grateful for the editorial assistance of Laura Gentile who read the entire collection and provided helpful feedback. Laura closely worked with me to improve all aspects of the book. I am grateful to her.

Rebwar Fatah
London, December 2016 for first edition
London, Updated September 2017 for the second edition
London, Updated April 2019 for the third edition

NALI

Nali (aka Mullah Khidir Ehmed Şawaysi Mîkayali 1797–1856) is one of the Kurdish classical poets whose name is usually associated with Salim (aka Abdul-Rehman Begi Saheb-Qiran, 1800-1866) and Kurdi (aka Mustafa Bagi Mahmud Bagi Sahebgran 1809-1850). They were the leading intellectual figures in the Kurdish Baban Principality (1649–1850). Nali was born in the village of Khakukhol, Sharazur, which is now part of the governorate of Sulaimaniyah,

Kurdistan; and he died in Istanbul. He was highly educated in religious studies. Apart from his native language, Nali knew Arabic, Farsi and Turkish. Not only was he a poet, but also a polymath, a linguist, a mathematician and theologist. He is one of two classical poets included in this anthology and below are two pieces by Nali which are considered to be representative of traditional Kurdish poetry.

The meter of this poem is mafayylum – mafayylum – fa'l or dad da dad da – dad da dad da – dad da. If one compares it to English poetic meters, one can state that the meter contains three feet. The original poem, same as almost all classical Kurdish poetry, possesses monorhymes in which all the rhymes follow the AA BA CA pattern to the end.

Winter Solstice

Is it the winter solstice or the darkest night, tonight?
When my sight, far from you, is without light, tonight.

My heart is like an ousted ruler, my love;
The gift of meeting you is looming tonight.

The heart is willing to see you, the reason of its
Wildness, lonely and far away from me, tonight.

While you are the Queen of Almond Eyes,
Why should I care for Caesar and the King, tonight?

Have your eyes woken up or are they always magical?
Have they always radiated or are they blessed, tonight?

My tears draw the shape of your eyes;

My place is that of Mansur[2], the victorious, tonight.

People ask about my situation;
I am headed towards the corner of loneliness, tonight.

I am leaving you

My friends, I am now leaving you;
Let the homeland be free from oppressed people.

You should walk town-by-town and village-by-village;
Escaping from friends, running around lands.

Do not say, "He was useless and left, who cares!"
My head is a shield, protecting you from disasters.

Because our journey is a fate-deciding one,
Pray for us, for you and your God's sake.

I am the head of your suffering army;
I fear; if I go, your army would be defeated.

Stop domesticating wild preys;
Just in case your prey may escape.

I merely kindly request; from time to time,
Remember your honest loved one.

---

2 Al-Mansur or Abu Ja'far Abdallah ibn Muhammad al-Mansur (714 AD – 775 AD) was the second Abbasid Caliph reigning accepted as the real founder of the Abbasid Caliphate.

KURDI

Kurdi (aka Mustafa Bagi Mahmud Bagi Sahebgran 1809-1850) is one of the Kurdish classical poets whose name is usually associated with Salim (aka Abdul-Rehman Begi Saheb-Qiran, 1800-1866) and Nali (aka Mullah Khidir Ehmed Şawaysi Mîkayali 1797–1856). He was born and died in Sulaymaniyah. Kurdi wrote in classical style very similar to Nali and Salim, but not many of his poems are available made it to the modern days.

It is Time for the Separation of Lovers

It is time to separate lovers, tonight
The breeze of disuniting icons blows, tonight

In the deserts of my chest, thorns of sorrow have grown
The clouds within my heart harvest grieving rain, tonight

Deep in my heart, I hear an echo, I think;
It is the chain clunking of old times, tonight.

The tears of a burned heart are sour;
It is the festival of drinkers, tonight.

When drops of tears fall on my heart,
It is the storms of my foes, tonight.

The red and yellow colours of my tears
Reveal the grief of a disturbed caravan, tonight.

My life and death pleasurably in unison depart and
Act like disappearing anxious people, tonight.

Do not prevent 'Kurdi' from grieving![3]
Resting is the habit of immoral people, tonight.

---

[3] It was customary for the Kurdish classical poets to put their pen name in the last verse of the poem.

ABDULLAH GORAN

The poetry of Abdullah Goran (1904 – 1962) greatly influenced the work of Kurdish poets that came after him. He is one of the most well-known Kurdish poets of the 20th century and there are plenty of reasons.

Goran was the first one who almost completely deviated from the Arabic *Aruz* rhythm. He wrote more poetry than his peers and he published his collections before all the others. Most significantly, his contemporaries gave up writing poetry, for various reasons, while Goran kept writing until his death. Goran was more effective in rendering the subject of his poems essential and striking.

Goran was born in Halabja, Sulaymaniyah, and studied in Kirkuk. Halabja was an intellectual centre at the time,[4] which was dominated by the noble Bagzaday Jaff clan, perhaps the most liberal and recipient clan known at the time, who established socio-political links with the British early at the turn of the 19th century.

Goran's ancestors were nobles from *Miran Bagi* who were originally from the region of Meriwan (aka: Mariwan, Marivan) in the Kurdistan region of Iran. As nobles, they had access to education that was not widely accessible to the common man. As most of the intellectuals of his generation, Goran had been introduced to religious studies at an early age at home, and was also taught by his father and in the Halabja local mosque. Thereafter, he became increasingly familiar with other people's languages and literature in the region, such as Farsi, Arabic and Turkish.

Goran and his companions made poetry available to ordinary people, greatly differing from their predecessors' work that could only be understood by the intellectual elite. Goran *et al* challenged the status quo to turn poetry into a language for and of the people whilst also remaining artistic. They assisted the establishment of a new school of Kurdish poetry. Many of Goran's poems have been turned into songs.

Goran not only composed but also translated poetry and he was generally gifted in various literary forms. Some of his prose was

---

[4] Halabja is known to the international community for being gassed by the regime of Saddam Hussein in 1988.

promoted in Kurdish publications at the time. Until 1954, Goran was the editor of the Kurdish journal *Zheen* (Life). In early 1959, he became the editor in chief of the journal *Shafaq* (Dawn), later known as *Bayan* (Morning). He was appointed as a lecturer at the department of Kurdish Language and Literature at the University of Baghdad in autumn of 1960.

During his lifetime, two of his poetry collections were published: *Paradise and Memory*, and *Tears and Art* in 1950. His complete collection was published, after his death, in 1980, which contained both previously published collections plus unpublished work.

Politically, Goran was an active member of the Iraqi Communist Party and paid the price under the oppressive regime. He was imprisoned in 1952 for six months. On November 17th 1954, Goran was arrested with a group of civil activists in Sulaymaniyah, where he was sentenced to one year in prison and one year of suspended sentence. He completed his sentence on September 12th 1956. On November 17th 1956, he was arrested as the result of his stance on Israel's attack on Egypt and was sentenced to a three-year imprisonment. He was released after the 1958 revolution on August 10th 1958.

In 1962, Goran was diagnosed with stomach cancer. He was treated in Baghdad and Moscow and returned to Sulaymaniyah where he passed away on November 18th 1962, at the age of 58.

Desire

There was a time, when the world of my soul, was dark and empty,
Even the sunshine in my soul was cold.
In the sky of my hopes, the stars –
Thousands of bright and beautiful regal stars,

Were submerged in a dark, black sea,
And engaged with death, just like broken flowers.

There was a time, when the gardens of my life, were without
music;
The nests of my nightingales were without songs;

My dreams were not dreams, my thoughts made no sense;
My feelings were like a disturbed ocean under heavy waves;

My soul was without strength so sad and depressed was I;
My hopes were dark, the death of my love was hidden within
the coffin of life.

I was hopeless; I thought that a fatal disease
Was bringing me the gift of death once and for all.

I thought I had to wait until careless nature
Encourages the bestiality of graves to devour me.

But my love, sweet love, my stunning lady;
With your rose red lips and dark black eyes;

With your tall figure, so supple and attractive;
With your sweet walks, graceful movements, and melodious
voice;

With all this exquisiteness in the beauty of heavens;
With all the magnificence that is in you;

From the first day that I saw the magic of your smile,

The nightingales of my soul began to sing;

The spring of my youth now flows once more;
The gardens of my life are filled with flowers;

Now, at least, your magic would occasionally
Become my melody – my sweet lady.

I vow to you, vow to attraction and vow to beauty,
All my senses will go back to what they once were.

The bright red blood flows through my veins,
The dark horizon of my sky will dawn.

It is passed! I would never grow old or my heart would face
death,
Or my bright happiness would be spoiled forevermore.

Now my love, my goddess, my Venus,
Don't permit the nightingale of my poetry to stop singing.

Lovers' Melody

Under the blue sky,
Within snow-covered peaks,
I have explored Kurdistan,
Searching valley by valley.

Neither in the towns nor in the villages,
Could I find anyone,
As exquisite as you.

There is only
One lovely Kurdish woman who makes me happy;
You are my fairy princess.

You are neither slim nor plump,
Neither a young nor mature woman,
Your eyes are not too black,
You are not too full of rosiness,
But for sweet looks,
I have not seen anyone else,
Who rivals your allure.
It is you alone,
That moonlight smiles suit,
For your walk is like a melody.

From the day that I saw you,
A love swept deeply into my heart.
If you are away for just one moment,
It is as if I am on fire.
When my hands cannot reach you,
My heart cannot rest with anyone else.
It is you alone,
The shelter of my dreams and hopes,
The vision of my precious life.

Before seeing you,
My life was bitter.
Without happiness or rest,
Without hopes or goals,
I felt homeless.
As if I had no one
To lead me onwards.

It is only you,
The guide of my hopes,
The one that makes my hard life easy.

You are a lovely woman,
As beautiful as Venus,
I worship you.
That is why I am ecstatic.
Some wonder about my religion,
But they should know,
It is you alone.

My religion and my faith,
The goddess of my vibrant heart's heaven.
As a fanatic for an objective,
I am neither *Kurmanji* nor *Zazaki*.[5]
I have explored all over Kurdistan,
Just like a nomad,
And nowhere could I find anyone
As beautiful as you.

It is only you, who is like the spring flowers,
A beautiful Kurdish woman.
Who else could revive Kurdistan?
In the entire sky, only morning star
Ignites beautiful feelings in my heart.

---

5 Two Kurdish speaking dialects

Beauty without a Name

A small instrument creates one thousand and one tunes;
The sweetest one to my ears is the quietest.

A clear water-spring shines in the moonlight;
In its bottom, diamonds of sand and pebbles shiver,

Is more appealing to me than the endless sea,
Whose waves roll and crash to the shore in the sunlight.[6]

Women and Beauty

I have watched stars in the sky;
I have picked flowers during spring;
My face was sprayed with dew of trees;
I have watched mountains during sunset,
A rainbow after a heavy rain
Has curved against the shining sun.
[...]
The throat of recorders and strings of violins
Have given many sweet tunes.
These are all beautiful and delightful,
Enlighten paths of life,
But even nature would never be
Bright without lover's simile.[7]

---

[6] Only selected verses were translated
[7] Only selected verses were translated

Bloody Flower

These are well-known lyrics by Abdullah Goran, but never created a libretto for them. The lyrics are powerful enough to bring a short musical, play or even an opera to life.

Goran identified two scenes for the play without an elaborate supporting text. I took the liberty of creating a supporting text and turned the provided material into a libretto that is ready to be adapted for a stage performance. The play consists of two scenes.

First scene:
The first scene is set in a beautiful village during autumn. Yellow leaves cover the ground. A young couple, man and woman, are standing far away from a house in the village. It is the venue of a

wedding. Everyone is dressed in colourful clothing and lots of couples are dancing. The young couple are engaged in a conversation. The young woman is beautifully dressed, wearing heavy jewellery.

On the other side, away from the village across a river, the huge castle of the king is visible. A narrow wooden bridge crosses over to the castle. Next to it flourishes a beautiful garden. The castle and the garden are heavily supervised by the King's unfriendly guards who are carrying old rifles.

Dialogue between the man and the woman:
The man looks at the woman with a smile while holding her hands and says:

Look! It is a wedding; people are dancing in that house
Listen to the sounds of zurna, drum and recorders!
Colours of red and yellow, men and women together, it is chaos.
The crowd is only missing the sounds of your jewellery.

The man gently pulls the woman's hand:

Please, hurry up, let us go and hold hands;
Let us with deep passion, join the dance.

The woman shakes her head and faces the man to respond:

If there are no flowers for my hair, one red and one yellow,
I shall not come to the party, I shall not dance.

The man desperately begs the woman to go and dance with him:

For the sake of your beauty, for the sake of your beauty, my love,

For the sake of your graceful walks to fetch water from the
village spring,
It is autumn; leaves have dropped; the gardens are bare;
There are no flowers, flowers have not blossomed with
smiles

The woman insists on having her hair decorated with flowers:

If there are no flowers for my hair, one red and one yellow,
I shall not come to the party, I shall not dance.
If you have given me your heart with all its meanings,
You would have picked two flowers for me from the garden
of the King.

*The man starts moving towards the King's garden despite the risk. He
is moving and singing. His voice slowly fading.*

The King's castle is on the other side of the river;
It is surrounded by a hostile clan.
If I go, my way is blocked, and I take a risk;
If I do not, my hazel eyes are angry.

*The man disappeared moving towards the garden. This ends the first
scene.*

Second scene:
The man is coming back from the King's garden and walks
towards the woman. He is carrying a beautiful fresh yellow flower
in his left hand and keeps his right hand on his heart. He looks very
weak and pale as he stands in front of the woman.

Man:

I searched the King's garden up and down;

I have found vivid yellow flowers, I picked one for you;
But I could not find red flowers, I am sorry.
I am not sure whether you will join me to dance.

Woman:

I am not coming; I still need one red flower for my hair.

Man:
*Then, the man moves his right hand from his heart and blood gushes
out of his wound, and says:*

Instead of a red flower, would you accept a fresh red wound
on my heart?

Woman:

What have I done? You have been shot by a hostile rifle!

*As the man collapses, she gives him her support. She is holding him as
she sits on the ground. Then she says:*

Lay down and for a short while put your head on my lap;
Let me cry for the heart that I lost for a flower.

AHMED HARDI

Ahmed Hardi (1922 – October 29th 2006) adheres to Goran's school of poetry, but he does have a unique style and almost all of his poetry is based on *Arud* except for a few poems which are compatible with Kurdish folk rhythm. Despite not having written extensively, modern Kurdish poetry has been significantly influenced by Hardi. His first collection of poetry was published in 1957 and a second edition was published in 1984. The second edition contained some new poems and updated renditions of some of the poems that were included in the original text. The writer's talent for weaving internal melodies into his poetry allowed his work to be turned into songs. Hardi wrote most of his poetry when he was young, which may explain why the themes of loneliness and disappointment are so omnipresent. Hardi was very selective with his poetry. He did not publish all of his work and only shared a part of it with the world, which is the reason why the size of his collection is rather small.

Hardi was born in the city of Sulaymaniyah in 1922. He worked as a primary school teacher in 1941. Towards the end of the 1940s, he lost his job due to his political stance. In 1959, along with some co-workers, Hardi established the political party, known as The Association of Free Resonance of Kurdish Unity (KAJIK). He joined the Kurdish armed movement soon after it started in 1974. When it collapsed in 1975, he and his family fled to Iran, living as refugees. He returns to his hometown Sulaymaniyah in 1979. In 1988, when the Kurdish armed movement rose again, he joined one of the Kurdish groups PASOK, working as the secretary general for a year. After 1989, he stayed as an independent individual in the Kurdish armed movement until the Kurdish uprising in 1991, and gave up his position in PASOK.

Hardi lived in exile in London from 1993 to early 2004. Following the ousting of Saddam Hussein's regime in 2003, he returned to his hometown. He passed away on October 29th 2006 in his city of birth, Sulaymaniyah.

I met Hardi as a teenager in the city of Sulaymaniyah, where he was teaching and also participating in literary meetings, which I used to attend. I was so impressed with Hardi's poetry, that to this very date I can recite all of his poetry in the first published collection, by heart. His poetry collection was out of print. I visited the local library and wrote all his poems by hand into a notebook, which I kept until I went to university. When I left after my studies, it got lost amongst many other things. However, when he lived in London, we grew closer as we were both a part of the small Kurdish community of London. We had many meetings where we discussed life, literature and his own poetry in general.

Lonely Secrets

A life of harsh sorrows has killed the butterflies of my desire,
Spilling the wine in the love glass of my youth.

The mist of bleak days has become so dark,
The love scenes of my heart are cloaked in despair.

Lonely nights have smothered the flames of my candle of hope,
The hopeless hands have strangled the euphoria of my innermost melodies.

And now, exposing the wounds
Of my unquiet emotions,
I wander in the mazes of my soul's wilderness.

In the dark nights of my loneliness, I retrace my steps blindly,
There is no hand that can rescue me from this abandoned grave.

There is no beauty to lend her soft heart to my troubled head,
Or to rest in exhaustion in her warm lap.

My weak eyes gaze, bewildered, into the dark nights.
There are no two bright eyes to illuminate my path.

Except for sorrowful wings
And frightening nights,
There is no light.

There is no single princess who urges me to desire,
Her secrets to revive my dying crumbled talent.

Her laughter to remove the gloomy fog from my eyes,
To consolidate me like a baby who for comfort cries.

Yes, when I listen, except for my distressed heart,
Which quietly reveals my deep and hidden mysteries.

There is no sound
Nowhere around,
Neither the beating of wings nor the sighing of a breath.

YUNIS REUF DILDAR

Yunis Reuf Dildar (February 20th 1918 – November 12th 1948), is well- known for writing the lyrics for the Kurdistan 'national' anthem, *Ey raqib* ('Hey, enemy') whilst he was in prison for his political activism. He was born in Koy Sanjaq or Koya, a small town in Iraqi Kurdistan, and soon his family moved to Raniya, another small town on the Iranian border, where he attended school. His father was a civil servant and soon he had to relocate with his family to Koya because of his job.

Koya, despite its size, is well-known for intellectual activities and is the birthplace of pioneers such as poet Haji Qadir Koayy and artists like Tahir Tofiq.

Dildar stated that from an early age, he knew the poems of many Kurdish poets by heart. His poetry collection was published in Erbil in 1959. Dildar used both Arabic *Arud* and Kurdish folk rhythm.

Dildar's first poem was published in 1935, the year that he graduated in Law at Baghdad University. He was a lawyer by profession. He tragically died at the young age of 30 in Erbil on November 12th 1948; hence he has not written many poems. He wrote "Hey enemy" in 1940. It is believed that Sheikh Hussein Barzinji conducted it.

"Hey enemy" consists of the *Arud* meter, *Fa'ylatun-Fa'ylatun-Fa'yln.*

Hey Enemy - the Kurdish National Anthem

Hey enemy guard! The Kurdish-speaking nation is alive,
Undefeatable by the weapons of all times.

Let no one say the Kurds are no more!
They are here and their flag never falls.

Our people have risen; they know no fear,
Ready to adorn the crown of life with blood.

We are the children of the Medes[8] and Keykhosrow[9].
Our faith and religion is the love for Kurdistan.

The Kurdish people have struggled for so long.
Look at our past - how red it is with blood!

The Kurdish youth has risen like lions,
To adorn the crown of life with blood.

Forever we will be ready to die;
For freedom and for loving our land.

---

8 The Medes believed to be an ancient people who lived in an area that is inhabited by Kurds today. They mainly inhabited the mountainous area of north-western Iran and the north-eastern and eastern region of Mesopotamia and the Kermanshah-Hamadan region. They emerged between 1000 BC to around 900 BC. It is accepted that Medes are related to Kurds.

9 Keykhisraw is a legendary king of the Persian Kayanian dynasty and a character in the epic Persian book "Shahnameh".

Kamaran Mukri

Kamaran Mukri (1929 – December 27th 1986), whose real name is Mohammed Ahmad Taha, is one of the more contemporary Kurdish poets and he was politically active as well. Between 1943 and 1963, he was imprisoned for six years by the Iraqi regime for his patriotic stance. Professionally, Mukri was a lecturer of Kurdish literature and language at the University of Sulaymaniyah. After the Baath regime closed down the university, he was moved to the University of Salahadin in Erbil, where he lived until he passed away in 1986.

Mukri published seven poetry collections: "Peace" (1954), "Gift" (1957), "Fire and Ember" (1958), "Poppy" (1959), "Fireflies" (1959), "Hope and Struggle" (1968) and "Power of Poetry" (1971). After his death in 1987, all of his poetry was collected and put together in one volume. He had his own style and predominantly used soft and musical vocabulary. Unlike other poets, he avoided using foreign words that have been diffused into the Kurdish language.

I met Mukri at the university of Sulaymaniyah during the 1970s when I was a student for four years. He did not teach me, as I did not study literature. I also met him during literary meetings in the city, where he was active.

Flowers

Flowers, with all their beauty,
Blossom in the laps of sharp thorns.

Hearts, to reach for their happiness,
Must taste the bitterness of life.

Hopes, embraced with regret and sadness,
Come true like the eruption of flower buds.

I don't Need Poetry

Your poetry is fine,
The daffodils of life;

Water springs for thirst;
Vineyards of hope and wonder;

Drops of squashed stars;
Tresses of sunlight.

Your poetry is sweet;
Like babies on a mother's lap;

High like mountain peaks;
Green like spring grass.

But my source of consciousness,
I am tired of poetry.

And don't search for fine poems;
For words from the heart,

I don't need poetry from you,
As I said, I only love you.

It was not the poetry you wrote,
It was only you who attracted me.

In Prison

Ask the prison and the Salman desert;[10]
The scars of the wounds on my shoulders.

---

10 Salman is short for the notorious Nuqra Salman prison in the deserts of
southern Iraq, which was mainly used for Kurdish and communist prisoners under
various Iraqi governments. Mukri was imprisoned here. In this poem, Mukri focuses
on his time and his condition within the prison.

Ask my youth, my tender age,
When life's opportunities were blazing with progress;
The years that I lived in chains.
During the avalanche that life forced upon me,
When I lived in confined rooms, paths of insects,
In damp walls and with angry guards and bleeding faces.

Ask the scabs on my body, shattered by flogging;
The continuously wrenching heart;
The fingers burnt by fire;
The dislocated joints.

Ask who my enemy was till yesterday,
Put fetters on hundreds like me.

Ask the handcuffs and shackles,
What I am and who I am; they know me well.

Ask the palm trees and burning deserts
The mirage, the scorching wind and my longing for water.

Ask the eyes that are used to being blood-filled;
The people whose only stake was punishment.
My baby, then, the focus of my desire;
My consciousness dying for a message;
One must forget the desire for fresh water
To calm the inner flames.

A glass of ice-cold yogurt of Kurdistan,
Wishing for breezes of shade in its woods.

Ask the hunger, exile and deprivation,

All clean wishes of the heart and soul.

Ask the handcuffs and shackles,
What I am and who I am; they know me well.

I am not a hero, neither well-known nor superior.
I am a poet who lives for Kurdish people.

Whatever I could, I did for my people and my homeland.
Whatever happened to me, I gave away with a careless smile.

My head is high; my feeling of surrender is low,
For which I sacrificed my peace and desire.

Ask the mountains, the high and low peaks,
The intense fire of my beliefs.

Ask the handcuffs and shackles,
What I am and who I am; they know me well.

Photograph

Oh, ray of sunlight; oh, bunch of flowers!
I held your photograph in my heart.

Though the wounds of my sad heart,
Do not heal with a photograph.

The flame of memories of old and new wounds,
Are always sore at the start.

Be safe! You have occupied my mind.
You have intensified the flame of my sadness.

The arrows of one thousand and one desires,
Hit my unlucky heart.

Why did you send me, my angel,
The photographs of distress and sadness faraway?

You have wounded my heart in many places.
How could l live with this pain?

ABDULLA PASHEW

Dr Abdulla Pashew (1946 - present) was born in Erbil, Iraqi Kurdistan, and in 1973 he moved to the former Soviet Union to study. He completed an MA degree in translation in 1979. In 1984, he accomplished his PhD on Kurdish literature; his focus being the Kurdish journalist, thinker and poet, Tawfeq Mahmoud Hamza, known as Piramerd (1867–1950). Pashew's work was deeply influenced by Piramerd and once I asked him about it and he replied: "I am Piramerdist." From 1985 to 1990, he was lecturing at a university in Libya. Since 1995, he has been living in Finland.

After decades in exile, it is hardly surprising that Pashew was influenced by Western literature; however, he developed and maintained his own poetic style. His early poems are mostly short but punchy. He has altered his style recently.

Pashew is known for his patriotic stance and for publicly opposing corruption. Pashew strongly believes in the Kurdish people's right to self-determination, and he is in pursuit of social justice.

He wrote his first poem in 1963 and his first poetry collection was published in 1967, entitled *Tear and Wound.* In 1968, his second collection *The Broken Sculpture* was published. Following this, further collections were published: *The night stories of a thirsty poet* (1972); *There is no a night I do not dream of you* (1980); *Kurdish internal conflict* (1994); *Twelve lessons for the children with some forbidden poems* (1997); *Sowing thunder* (2000); *Towards sunset* (2001); and, *The sack of a native lover* (2006).

All of his poems were collected in several of volumes recently.

Peshaw was a friend of my late brother, Dilshad Meriwani, and he used to visit us at home. I also met him several times in Europe, after I left Kurdistan.

Aimless

I hide you in vain;
If another is near, I shall remain silent with you.
Whatever secret that is not revealed,
Sooner or later,
I shall reveal it in a poem.

What a Pity

The friends,
Who were once
The source of my peace of mind,
The sweet guests,
Of my always open heart.

Now,
They are either
Wiped out or almost faded away,
From my memory.

And yet,
I still wait for the gazelles,
They promised to arrive,
But never did.

Dew

You are a drop of dew,
On the leaves of the spring of life.
You, my love, lady of the stars;
I fear to approach you,
You may fall down to earth.

You are Saddened

You are saddened,
By the widows;
By the widowers;

By the orphaned babies.

I am even more saddened,
For those warriors and angels,
Who, for years, were expected to be born,
But never were.

Pearls

If the sea had a choice,
It would give its riches to the wave.
If the wave had a choice,
It would give its riches to the shore.
But only occasionally,
The wave wins a pearl;
It offers it to a shore.

Do not rush me!
I am merely a sea wave,
Restless, unstable, always on the move.
Seldom has the sea granted me a pearl.
Yet, I offer it to you.

At the Funeral of a Poem

My head was like an ocean;
Sharp thoughts, like fish,
Floated
And submerged;
Until morning when I cast the net,
I caught a fish.

After a few tosses and turns,
Even she gasped and expired.

Halabja

I should not be surprised, here and there,
In the Kremlin or the White House,
To see some human beings,
Who instead of nails have claws;
Instead of teeth have fangs,
But it would be shocking,
Just like God's miracles
Have two eyes and walk upright on two legs.

Dissolving

I see through you;
I hear through you;
I talk through you.
Unfortunately,
The fame is mine and you are no one.
How unjust I feel: it is well-known,
That you are not me but somebody else!

Lustre and Candle

Before writing,
Some need a magnificent lustre,
To find the way to the Sultan's heart.

Before writing,

Some need a simple candle,
For self-reflection and burning darkness.

Before stretching my hand to pick up my pen,
I examine
Whether the light
Comes from the magnificent lustre or the simple candle.

Treasure

Since the beginning of the earth,
Man has loved pearls and
Sought silver and gold;
Combing the depths of oceans;
Scaling the peaks of mountains.
But, every morning,
I discover a treasure,
When I see your braids
Covering half my pillow.

Sleepless

Tonight, as other nights,
The wild gazelle of my sleep has fled,
The grass plains in my eyes.

Your happiness is a treasure,
I fear, it could be stolen.
To keep it safe;
I remain awake!

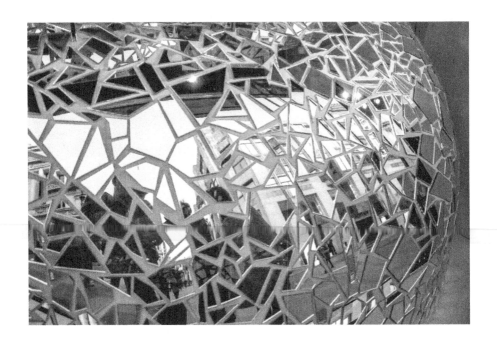

If I Had an Apple

If an apple were to fall into my basket,
I would cut it in half.
I would keep one half
And offer you the other.

If I smiled;
I would share most of it with you.

If I grieved;
I would never share it with you.
Until my last breath,
I would keep it to myself.

Youth and Old Age

Whatever I do, I cannot separate,
Youth and age;
I worship both.
At dusk, I honour the twilight;
At dawn, I honour the sunrise;
Awed, I bow my head.

Masterpiece

I have many different poems:
Some are towns;
Some are villages;
Some are castles; and
Some are tiny and in ruins.

But the poems that I have written for you
Will become masterpieces
And the brightest capitals on Earth.

To a Gypsy

Don't look at my palm anymore!
I don't want you to tell me,
How many children I will father;
Whether I will be rich or stay poor.
Just tell me one thing,
Will I live as you live, as long as I am alive?
Or I shall have a homeland?

Snowstorm

I witnessed a snowstorm at dusk,
When I made my palm a nest
For a wandering snowflake.
I watched it with passion
As it melted.
When it turned into water.
I could see it.
In Kurdistan,
It was a drop of spring dew.

Silence

When I am silent,
Do not talk to me!
Do not shake the branches of my mind
Until its berries ripen.

I am not the only silence;
See how the mountains stay silent,
When they expose their chests
To the sword of lightning.

Look how the grass keeps silent;
When it stretches its blades
Towards the light.

When I am silent,
Do not imagine that I am free and carry no burdens;
Just as the bees, I am busy.

I told you so much about the homeland,
Until your heart fills with her love.
You hope to visit even once,
To see her villages and her towns,
To touch her wounds.

When I am silent,
Saddle my silence.
Look at me and strike the stirrup!
See my homeland,
Through me.

Parting

Every night, when the pillow
Invites our heads;
As the two poles of the earth
To the feast of sorrow,
Separation arrives to lie between us.
Shining, like a dagger,
I remain awake.
Staring with open eyes,
I wonder whether you see as I do.

Every night, when the pillow
Invites our heads;
As the two poles of the earth;
To the feast of sorrow;
My heart stands helpless, like a ball
To be hit.

I fear to die before you;
I will lose my mind if you die before me.

Habit

Every day, early morning,
I fill my heart
With the rays of the sun;
With the electric red current.
As a letter, I wrap it up,
To release it to the wind.
The wind is free to take it.
I don't ask,
Where it would be taken to!

I Love You Both

As I live only once,
I love you both.

As I live only once,
I neither offend the sunlight
Nor the moonlight.

If I lived twice, however,
I would have loved you in this life;
And in the other,
I would have kept my love for her.

As I live only once,
I have no choice!

I love you both,
I worship both
The sunshine and the moonlight.

Dream

I cannot sleep.
I am afraid,
That as soon as I leave you,
I may lose you.
Our remaining days are very few,
And can be counted on the fingers of one hand;
Like a few drops of dew,
Under the blazing sun.

I cannot sleep.
My love, sleep!
Imagine a sea,
As calm as your eyes.
Think of a sky,
As quiet as my pain.

Don't be sad!
Be calm and sleep!

Last night, I had a sweet dream;
Man had a thousand hands;
On each hand
Thousands of fingers blossomed.

Confession

The sun wanders across the sky till evening,
But it never loses sight of the horizon.
The river comes across thousands
Of crooked paths,
But it never loses its way to the sea.

In the interval,
Between our parting and meeting,
I may come across embraces,
But all of them point the way to you.

Mother

For Jamila[11], I bow in respect;
For Joan of Arc and Tereshkova[12],
I kneel before their greatness.
But in my land of death,
A woman dares to give birth to a child,
In front of her, I fall upon my knees,
And let my forehead touch the earth!
I worship her.

The Extreme Thirst

I kiss you.
My sweet love, I kiss you.
I kiss your neck,
Your ears,
I suck both your nipples.

I am truly thirsty,
Although I know your breasts
Are like salty seawater.
The more I suck them,
The more
The dry yellow trees of thirst
Strengthen within my bones.

---

11 Jamila, or Djamila Bouhired, was an Algerian woman who opposed the French colonial rule. Jamila was regarded as the face of the Algerian revolution.

12 Valentina Vladimirovna Tereshkova (March 6th 1937 - present) is the first woman to have flown in space. She is a retired Russian cosmonaut and politician.

You are my soul.
In the first course of love,
Your breasts have taught me
To respect the snow atop the mountains.
Your eyes taught me
To respect the springs in the valleys.

I wish I could go back to my school desk
To wait for you.
In the second course of love,
Learn to protect your breasts,
Learn to guard your eyes.

Before the Thunder

We can make winter come late.
And when it arrives,
It can arrive without storms or snow.

We can make the stormy sea,
As calm as the sky.
And we can make the sky as deep as the sea.

If you ever decide to destroy the temples,
I wouldn't try to change your mind;
I would bring you an axe.

If you ever decide to destroy the nest,
I wouldn't beg you not to;
I would bring you the stones.

But before you raise the axe,
Before you destroy the soft nests,
I will tell you,
It is not too late
To delay winter.
And when it arrives,
It can arrive without storms or snow.

Your Eyes

If I were lost in the dense forest;
If my boat went missing adrift a raging sea
And capsized,
I would not be afraid;
As long as your eyes are my guide,
As long as your eyes are my nearest port.

Others listen to the media
For the weather forecast.
But when the evening comes,
I look deep into your eyes.
They tell me from where the wind will blow,
The intensity of the heat,
In which fields, forests and mountains
The rain will water.

Prophecy

I am not a fortune teller.
I do not read books of destiny,
Nor the lines of fate on the palms of hands.

Yet, it is clear to me.
And I know as long as you love me,
You will remain a soft melody
That is sung by gypsies
On winter nights.

You will become a verse,
In the morning the sun will write you.

At the sunset,
The enemies of poetry
Bury you in a grave.

Authority

My pen is a hammer.
Each of my words a nail.
Wherever oppression exists,
I pierce it like softwood.

A Word about my Heart

My heart is like those trains
That visit a thousand and one stations;
And stopping at each of them,
Leaving a passenger behind
And picking up another.

But since my heart became a train,
It carries one sad passenger
Who never absconds.

He stays on, searching:
For himself,
For his name,
For his eyes.

This passenger is my eternal wound.
This passenger is my eternal joy and sorrow.
This passenger is my Motherland.
Named Kurdistan, the cradle of my first love.

Without You

Without you,
I am a dot
That wanders in a huge orbit.

But with you,
The universe is reduced
To the size of a tiny ring
To fit the word of a poem.

Occasional Sadness

Occasionally sadness attains the peak,
And the pain reaches such an extent,
That I wish to hurl my life against a rock;
To be splashed
The way a glass of wine is smashed.

But suddenly,
The gleam of a fresh idea,

An intense notion,
The rebirth of a blade of grass,
The burst of a baby's laughter,
The perfect figure of a woman,
The quivering of a woman's breast,
Reward me with wings of happiness,
And make me berate God;
For making the bridge of my life so long,
That in centuries I will not cross over it!

Criterion

I am never against dictators
Invading the world;
To be the shadow of God

And increase the population.
But I have one criterion,
Children must not be dictators.

Madness

I know you are just a word,
But often, for a simple word,
I sacrificed an entire poem.

I know you are just a flower bud,
But often, for only one bud,
I left a garden of roses behind.

The Burned Forest

Any beauty who lent me her heart,
I planted her love like a sapling
Within reach of my soul's mountain;
Until it reached a point,
Of me possessing a vast forest,
Thanks to love!

When I met you, tender sapling,
I thought you would join others:
You shall grow;
In the heat of summer
I take pleasure in your shade;
In the depths of winter
I seek out your heat.

But suddenly, your spark
Turns my forest to ashes.

The Free World

The free world
Has heard enough
About the pulse of oil deep in the earth's heart.
It has become crippled,
Stone-deaf and blind
It doesn't feel the mountains burning.

Internal Conflict

At night in my dream,
I saw Haji's[13] final resting place
I knelt down courteously.
I said, "Haji, I am nervous."
He lowered his head,
And put his hand on his heart to say,
"Do me a good deed! Bring me back to life!"
I said, "Good Lord, I am not Jesus.
How could I bring you back to life? Please tell me!"
He said, "Take me out of here,
And bury internal conflict in my place!"

---

13 Haji Qadiri Koyi (1816 - 1897) was an influential and patriotic Kurdish poet.

Letter

It is evening,
It drizzles slowly.
I am lonely,
Perhaps not.
All of Moscow is in my steps.
The loneliness was a gazelle
Running from a hunter;
I cannot reach her anymore.

It is evening.
It drizzles slowly.
I am lonely,
Perhaps not.
I am walking.
The streets
Tie themselves to my legs.
I am walking.
In my pocket
Is a letter in a red envelope.
It beats,
Just like my second heart.

Soothing

Do not worry about the poems
I have written for other beauties.
Deep inside each of them,
I now see only you.

My heart is as dark
As a forgotten cave.
Light a simple candle;
Draw me closer to you.
Press your cheek to my chest
In the same way that Kurds are one with their mountains.

I wish to assure your emerald eyes.
I wish to vow
That I don't see any others in you.

To a Cold Beauty

I admit,
You are delicate
Like a dewdrop on a petal.

You are a temple for all eyes,
Like a dewdrop on a petal.

You have become my passport.
We are always together, and yet I am bored of you.

I am a highlander.
The slightest touch,
Like a flame, brings my blood to boil.

And yet you are ice-cold,
Just like a dewdrop on a petal.

Poetry

The more I live, the more I love poetry.
As poetry is a capricious woman;
Every day,
We agree on our dating place.
Alas, she arrives rarely or not at all.

You Will Leave Me Too

You will leave me too.
I know you will.
I know it too well.
As a drink
Has left behind an empty bottle,

You will leave me too.

You will leave me too:
As the greenery departs the gardens,
As the clouds depart the mountains,
You will leave me too.

You will leave me:
As a swift horse escapes the warrior,
As fine words escape innumerable lips,
You will leave me too.

If you know,
This time,
Your decision is final.
Change your address,
Wipe out our footprints;
Under the sky of this town,
Only then can I say,
Goodbye
To you.

Leave me:
Like a swift horse
Escapes the warrior,
Like fine words
Escape innumerable lips,
Leave me.

SHERKO BEKAS

Sherko Bekas (May 2nd 1940 – August 4th 2013) was born in the city of Sulaymaniyah to a financially modest family. His father, Fayaq Bekas, a teacher by profession, wrote poetry that resonated the hardship of the locals. Bekas was introduced to poetry at a very young age.

Bekas was one of the founders of the socio-political *Rwanga* literary movement in the early 1970s.

He joined the Kurdish armed movement in the early 1980s and after its collapse, he moved away to Sweden and lived there from 1987 to 1992. After the establishment of the Kurdistan Regional Government in northern Iraq, Bekas returned to Kurdistan to take up the post of the minister of culture, from which he resigned shortly after.

In 1998, with the financial support of the Kurdistan authorities, he established the Sardam Publishing House and remained the managing director until his death. His first poetry collection, *The Moonlight of Poetry*, was published in 1968. His entire poetry collection was published in eight volumes in 2009.

Despite the publication of all his collections, Bekas preferred his poetry to be recited; and he did so himself, sacrificing hours to the deed. Bekas left an invaluable legacy of recorded poetry behind.

Bekas passed away in a hospital in Stockholm, having suffered from cancer. Following his request, he was buried in the public park *Parki Azadi* in Sulaymaniyah.

Bekas was a friend of my late brother and I knew him personally. We met on numerous social occasions and during his poetic events.

God's Response to Halabja

After suffocating Halabja,
I wrote to God,
A long letter of complaint.

Before reading it to the people,
I recited it to a tree.
She was in tears.

A bird-post on the tree, asserted:

Who is going to deliver your letter?
Don't you expect me to go over!
l cannot reach the heaven of God.

Late at night,
The mourned Angel of my poetry
Told me:
Don't you worry!
I'll deliver your letter high up for you,
But, I can't promise that God will receive it in person.
You see, our God Almighty can never be seen.
I said:
That is fine; now I wish you to fly high.
My poetry Angel took off with my letter.

When she came back, the day after,
A note was written
At the end
By the fourth junior Secretary of Almighty:
Idiot be fair; translate the note into Arabic!
No one speaks Kurdish around here.[14]

To the Western Kurds

To the Kurds of my heart,
To the Kurds of my soul,
To the Western Kurds,
To the peace of my conscience,

---

[14] Bekas wrote this poem to honour the memory of Halabja. Over 5,000 people were gassed on March 16th 1988 by the regime of Saddam Hussein in this town. Islamic groups issued a *fatwa* (religious decree) for his death as a result of this poem.

To the peace of my own existence,

Now, children are rolling in their blood, there,
And yet, my leader halts the supply of milk.

Now, the old and ill amongst my people are unable to flee;
As my leader barricades their escape routes. [15]

In This Colourful Region

In this colourful region of mine,
The unsighted
Can see fine,
The thieves one by one,
Whether by daytime or in clear moonlight.
And yet, they all escape
The clear vision of
Parliament Members
And ministers.

Now a Woman is my Homeland

Good morning!
My name is Wall,
Situated on the main street.
I am stretched as long as fury.

---

[15] Bekas wrote this poem when the Kurdish leadership of Iraq decided to close the border with Syria, not allowing Syrian Kurds in need to save their lives by fleeing to Iraq. Bekas used 'Western Kurds' for 'Syrian Kurds'. This is a common name among the Kurds.

I am as tall as anger.

Every slogan is stuck on me,
Every poster is pinned to me.
Amongst one hundred slogans,
Not one teaches me anything.
Amongst one hundred posters,
Not one makes me happy.

It was only yesterday,
From the top of my head to the tips of my toes,
Slogans were stuck on me.
When I read them,
I was embarrassed.

I am a wall of such a country,
Such big fat lies
Are distributed on me. [16]

For Sakine, Fidan and Leyla

A tree said:
We cannot name a street in Diyarbakir
After you now.[17]

A flower said:
We cannot name a garden in Qamishli[18]

---

[16] This is an extract from a poem recited by Bekas. The entire poem takes a couple hours to recite.

[17] Sakine Cansız, Fidan Doğan and Leyla Söylemez were three female Kurdish dissidents from Turkey, who were assassinated in France.

After you now.

A poem said:
We cannot name a public library in Sablakh[19]
After you now.

A rock said:
We cannot name a sculpture
Created on the chest of Babagurgur[20]
After you now.

Then, Kurdistan said:
What we can do now is only that;
Just like flower, poetry and freedom,
Carry you in our souls.

New Iraq

Yes, it was me, myself;
I rebuilt the demolished gallows;
And delivered them, on my shoulders,
To re-erect them in front of the gates of Baghdad
Yes, it was me, myself;
I warmed up,
The hibernated poisonous snake
Of this Iraq,

---

[18] Qamishli is a Kurdish city in Syria, now known as Rojava.

[19] Sablakh is the old name of the Kurdish city Mahabad situated in the Kurdistan region of Iran.

[20] Babagurgur is the area where oils flow out in Kirkuk, a city in the Kurdistan region of Iraq.

To gain strength;
To paralyse my heart.

2000 Images, 2000 Words, 2000 Years

At the turn of the millennium, Kurdish artist, Dr Rebwar Saed, painted 2000 paintings, one for each year of the last 2000. Sherko Bekas wrote a 2000-word poem for the paintings, one word for one year. At the time, I translated parts of Bekas' poem and provided an introduction to it. The entire work, Saed's paintings, Bekas' poetry and my translation were exhibited in London. I have provided my share of the project.

How can one tell a story of the last 2000 years? This is the question that Saed and Bekas must have asked themselves before embarking on this challenging project. Many directions could have been taken and none of them would have been easy. How much history can be captured in one image or word? Not much, one would think. But as it appears, both Saed and Bekas were successful. A framework for one image is limited – but imagination is not – and imagination is what Saed relied upon. Saed's challenge was to capture that imagination in art.

Saed took on a unique technique called 'trying his luck'. He 'spilled' paints of different colours onto his work sheet and then tried to identify an image out of the shape. Saed may have tried his luck with the colours, but he still needed to identify images that represented that specific year of history. Every identification was directly related to the richness of his own imagination. What else could he do? How could he encompass all the stories that were to be found within the time frame of 2000 years? These were the questions that he faced early in this challenge. Isn't that what history is made of?

Random interactions of phenomena appear as a nature ruled by laws to humans or perhaps humans try to make sense out of nature. This may have been the case for natural history, but human history is intelligent, hence more conscious. Humans engineer life today. Saed has engineered fascinating images to reflect each historical year.

The 'spilling' technique has given the images a unique feature; they appear to be washed out. Isn't that reflecting what history is? These images are mostly human heads that are mixed-up with animals, plants, scripts, castles, homes and other objects to symbolise that they all shared and shaped 2000 years of history together.

The beauty of this collection lies therein that Saed did not rely on images of ruling classes (e.g. sheikhs, kings and queens) to give time-identity to the images, but on the historical objects that have grown from an interaction of both human and natural history. For example, Saed has used domestic animals (fish, birds...) houses and castles to contextualise the images historically. Saed does not undermine human achievements during the past 2000 years. He ingeniously has mixed Kurdish-village-style homes with human heads, sometimes right on top of the heads, as if to imply that these achievements are the creation of human imagination. By mixing human heads with other objects, Saed implies that during the process of changing our environment, we have changed too. These are not static images. Saed has made them dynamic by, for example, mixing a pigeon with a human head to add the time-dimension into the image.

2000 words for the third Millennium
Bekas has described this history in a more general form:

"This is the story of water, laughter of water and crying of water,
In the path of 2000 rivers on the face of earth.
It is a story of stones, yelling of stones,
From the first hours when the earth started breathing."

Bekas has related this to human and natural suffering:

"Pain is moving around life
It is a story of wind and the songs of wind that spill colours
It is the shouting of earth and yelling of nature when
humans are born and when they die."

Now it is time to link the contribution of his nation to human history:

"This is the story of my past and present face;

Only one face but 2000 branches of my sights,
Only two eyes but 2000 views.

This is my magical language.
It is my calling while water crystallises.
This is the age of Iceland, age of fog.
This is the age of my decapitated head.

   Rotating the globe around me:

From the valleys of sunny small Asia,
A red beam falls onto the labs of the stony mountains.
When Zoroast writes his laws with fire,
"Mezda" beam souls,
"Ahriman" beam sounds of pain and wounds.
The Meds were the wings of power as they rise to the
mountains."

   In this manner, Bekas describes the birth of the Kurdish/Iranian
Zoroastrian religion. But this glorious epoch did not last long, as
Islam invaded Kurdistan to massacre and destroy. As fire was
sacred in this religion, Bekas symbolises Islamic destruction by
putting fire out and passionately saying:

"The hearths fall down the mountains and the Atishga get
cold[21]
The holy bird flies; the faces put out and the sky runs down
on me
I cover under the fog of the year
And I lose my Gods.

----

[21] Atishga is the name for a Zoroastrian place of worship.

Then Bekas describes the suffering of Kurds and Kurdistan under the swords of Islam. He symbolises Islam by sand, coming from the desert.

"My voice does not reach any God. My views produce thorns.
The views become the roads for swords that attack from the desired,
They attack the body of my words,
The remains of my last hopes and my last Atishga.
The desert swallows my mountains,
The desert brings dust with a new mission."

He describes those years:

"Every year was a sword to decapitate my voice.
Every year was fire to burn the snow off my body.
Every year was torture that was revolving around my head and my hands,
And shrouded me with blood and death.
Every year appeared as "Khalifa" to present the gales of hatred."

Bekas remarkably goes on to the oppression of Kurds in a different epoch:

"Wherever I turn, a tree of pain grows;
Wherever I whisper, a flame of Hell arises;
Wherever I spill my colours, a bird of death lifts off.

One, two and three centuries, I lit lights in my blood.
One, two and four centuries, I become a shattered love; I am scattered smoke;
A tangled web of thousands of years of pain and suffering.

Open your head, and the death of forests spills out;
Open your heart, and gardens of death blossom."

Bekas ends his 2000 years by looking for a new philosophy to progress his mission in the 3rd millennium:

"Years have died, and years have been born.
In the third millennium,
I take the first steps towards fresh words; my sounds
surprise me.
I stand in front of the first mirrors; my colours surprise me.
At dawn, I mix imagination with colours.
I attempt to bring a sound into my poetry that has not been
heard before;
I attempt to bring a colour into my painting that has not
been seen before."

Then, he regards himself powerless in this complex dilemma, so he seeks refuge amongst new generations:

"I must borrow the dreams of childhood
And ask, ask and ask again."

DILSHAD MERIWANI

Dilshad Meriwani (March 28th 1947 – March 13th 1989), whose full name is Dilshad Mohammed Amin Fatah, was a contemporary Kurdish writer, actor, novelist and poet. He was my eldest sibling. As an outspoken journalist and writer, he was detained by Saddam's security forces on February 12th 1989, to be executed on March 13th 1989. No one knows exactly what happened inside Meriwani's cell. All we know is that he died of two bullet wounds to the head. The only information surrounding his execution was his death certificate, as his body was never returned or recovered. Some former inmates who were lucky enough to be released, provided some information about him. For example, one inmate stated that when Meriwani arrived, the environment of the cell totally changed, as he kept the inmates engaged and entertained. He started exercise programmes and he drew a chessboard on the concrete floor. He also created the chess pieces out the soft inside of bread rolls.

Meriwani was arrested several times during his life, including in 1963, when he was only 16.

Meriwani wrote in an exquisite language. Some of his poems have become well-known songs. I found the way he expressed himself at such an early age fascinating. His early poetry is rather romantic. Later in his life, especially during the 1980s, his style had changed because he became more dedicated to the Kurdish political cause. In his first collection, *Tears and Smiles*, published in 1968 – at the age of 21, Meriwani's poetic talent can be sensed as his command of the language is strong. Subsequently, his other collections were published: *The first step* (1973); *Turn to light* (1976) and *The symphony of flowers* (1980).

He was also active in other fields of literature and art. His published collections of short stories are: *I see you with my figures* (1977); *Der Yasin* (1978) and *The lovers of revolution* (1973). *The welcoming of his majesty* was published in 1973, a comparative piece on two stories written on the same subject by two authors. Meriwani acted in two plays, in 1973 and 1974. He translated a high number of poems by international celebrities such as Muzafar Nawab, Samih Qasim, Paplo Neroda, Mhamud Darwish, Vladimir Mayakovsky, Constantine P. Cavafy and others.

Meriwani has contributed both poems and Robayyat to this collection. He stated that he wrote these during 1964-5, when the Iranian poet and mathematician Omar Khayyam inspired him. The influence of Khayyam is prominent in Meriwani's Robayyat.

To My Friends

I know I will be murdered;
And my body will be discarded on a wasteland.
It will be deformed to an extent,
Beyond recognition.

No one will know;
Whether it is the body of a human trafficker,
Or of an outlawed prophet.

My friends will not recognise me.
They will not recognise:
My unfortunate appearance,
My unbowed figure,
The hopes in my bright eyes,
My wounds,
The torture maps on my body,
My active eyebrows,
My looking for future lips.
My friends cannot recognise me.

Despite that all my friends, with a sigh;
Look at my discarded body on the wasteland,
And ask each other:
Why have I not been eaten by wild dogs?
Why have I not been eaten by hungry dogs?
Why have they not even touched me?

My friends,
Even if my body was bitten by dogs;
It would not be bites of hungry or wild dogs.

They don't bite me.
It is only the security dogs that deform me.
And that is why, I have kept intact.
And my enemies could not stand against me.

Concerned Meeting

Your eyes are two bright and soft halls;
They host the world's biggest meeting of sorrow.
Your lips are two red, thin ribbons;
Tie the world's biggest flower bunch of sorrow.

You are my concerns.
I can never give up;
Worshipping your eyes and lips,
Because I am like the permanent head of the meeting;
Because I am like the vase of the flower bunch.
I am seen by those two eyes.
I am kissed with those two lips.

Love

I am too,
Just like you,
Imperfect.
And yet I still love you.
And yet you still love me.
I suffer,
When I lose you, I'll be annihilated.
You suffer,
When you lose, you'll be destroyed.

Often, I feel,
Your love
Is a big red ant,
It crawls over my body.
Grain after grain,
Transfers all my body cells
To your body.
When I realise,
You are me
And I am still myself,

Often, I feel
The souls of people around me.
Like red bricks, one-by-one, I lay them down,
On the building of my own life.
Till I build a sacred castle.
And then,
When I look around,
I am no longer 'I'
I become 'They'.

Often,
I listen to Ali Mardan.[22]
I cry.
I feel that I am in love
With a Kurdish woman.
When I wander into the markets,
Not only one woman,

---

[22] Ali Mardan was a prominent Kurdish composer, singer and expert on *Maqams*, a specific Kurdish and Iraqi music.

I see men and women.
And I realise
Not only a woman,
I am in love with
All Kurds.

Don't Blame Me!

My sweetheart,
I am sorry.
Before passing away,
You did not have time to cry.
Close your eyes and sleep, as much as you may.
Don't blame me for shedding tears;
I am dismayed:

The shrapnel pieces of the grenade,
I felt in your chest
Were made in a factory
That was licensed to produce children's toys,
With which one day, ours could have played.[23]

Birth

The morning that your partner was in labour,
You were sad to leave her with the nurses.
And you left home,
To see the children attend their schools.
You attended the factory.
The machines start moving,
When they come in contact with your fingers.

In the evening, you come back home exhausted,
But delighted.
The children have learnt a new word;
And you had a newly born baby.

Soft Telegraph

When I miss you,
I feel,
I am a mythical lover,
Without home or a shelter.
For as long as this planet
Orbits around the sun,

---

[23] This is an extract from a longer poem.

I will orbit around you.

The Fortieth Year

The pen and paper under my hand
Are engaged in restless kissing.
They sacrifice each other.[24]

The croaking of a frog;
The crowing of a rooster;
Knock on the window of my room;
The hands of the thirty-ninth leave my embrace,
Leave the rendezvous for the fortieth year.
The fortieth year like a vine full of bunches of experience
Opens her arms for me,
Climbs over my body.

Life is in flames again;
The flame of disappointment and optimism;
The flame of a troubled life addicted to concerns.

My neighbouring night-woman is showing her client the
way out.
She will be lonely just like myself.
The last programme of my radio next to me,
Says goodbye to the listeners.
It will be lonely, just like me.
The nest of the two birds, just outside my room,

---

[24] Meriwani wrote this poem the night he turned 40 years of age. He was
executed just under two years after writing this poem.

Start grieving songs, just like my heart.
They will be restless.
Although the criminal black paws of a wild cat cannot reach
them,
But destroy the two eggs, which they have been sitting on
for days.

The dawn opens the button of a thick foggy day of my life.
I can hear the walking of two lonely people.
The steps of the first do not follow the second.
They are in the living room.
I can hear them; they hung up to ask for each other's help.
The footsteps halt, to start with the sound of eating an
apple.

The last glass of my drink,
Catches my lips to kiss me goodbye.
The sound of the apple being eaten mixes with the sip of my
drink,
Makes me tipsy.

For a minute, in the living room, I can hear a baby cry
I stand up to disengage the door latch:
A sharp toothed lizard wishing me a happy fortieth birthday.

My beautiful lizard,
The dream of the two birds will not be untrue.
One day, it will come true.
Today the birds live in a nest of fear,
But tomorrow, they will lay two new eggs.

Haji Mahmud

Haji Mahmud,[25]
Had no sons or daughters.
He was not even married.
He had neither sisters nor brothers.
He had no one.

Haji Mahmud,
Had a dream.
When he wakes up the next morning,
He decides to donate to a charity, to please his God.
He pays seven times,
But he still fears
To touch his morning egg.
He says: today I only have
A slice of bread with my cup of tea.
I fear from my egg,
A baby Baathist may hatch.

Death is Unfortunate

When the night comes, being lost is not what I am.
Being lost knows of me.
Being lost follows my steps.
Being lost stands in my way.
Being eccentric and a lover;
Being boring pains;

---

[25] Haji Mahmud is a common name for a man. Meriwani used the name as a symbol for an ordinary person.

Chasing death away;
Eliminating grief and sorrow.
I know who I am, I know my ways,
I know my end and my last resting place.

How about you, Death, the killer waiting down my road.
I know, you are harvesting my head,
But what would you do after my death?
Who else would you enjoy beheading
Like you enjoy the loss of mine?

I laugh over the sickle in your hand;
You are unfortunate!
What would you do after my death?

Reassurance

I returned,
I leave my luggage of sorrow
In front of your door.
I knock on it.
I rest my head on the luggage
And stay in the storm.
Your voice is my only meal.
The door takes hold of you,
To pass it to me.
Whether you open the door or not,
I am reassured that I shall not die.
Be reassured,
My luggage shall not become my grave.

Meriwani's Robayyat

1
When the moon was invaded, Khayyam smiled:[26]
Now humans have climbed onto the moon.
Before, I worried for one world only;
Soon, I will have to be concerned for two.

2
I drink wine from a flower-bud.
I drown my pains and sorrows in it.

The dark night that disturbs life,
With her soft kisses, I ease it out.

3
My lifesaver is a bottle of wine;
It is the grape juice of this Kurdistan.
The bottle shattered, when my vineyard burned,
Though, I am still happy tomorrow will turn.

4
The first sip of wine tastes bitter;
But the second annuls the first.
Go on to the third, the head is tipsy;
You may be real old, act as a baby.

5
We are all guests on this planet;
Hospitality is short, merely a moment;
I know that guests deserve some respect;
We are alike, merely two guests.

6
A fearless life is given to me;
Nature has offered for its pleasure.
Why does death have to intervene? What's the reason?
After I've tasted the bitter life.

7
I wish the poppy of my tender age
Could have revived, after it faded;
If this was the case, in the other life;
I would have destroyed the seven heavens.

8

Where I come from - does puzzle me.
Where I am heading - is unresolved.
Why I do exist - has not been addressed.
Let me have a glass before it all ends.

9

I've seen it, all the way through.
I've never heard gifts reclaimed.
God Almighty has offered life;
After giving it, he wants it back.

10

The secret of life is too complex.
Man may not be able to reveal it.
Pour me wine, as I have a real fear:
That even this glass may not reach my lips.

11

I've read dogmas of wise men;
No one could help me to reach the end.
Beating around 'whys' and 'hows'.
I'm yet to hear, "This is the reason!"

12

You love or hate me, I only love you,
For keeping me in your mind.
I only hate who doesn't know me;
And who forces me out of his head.

13

Life is today, tomorrow is false;
You shouldn't miss the joy of today.
Drink wine, warm your heart;
Who says, you'll have warmth tomorrow.

14

Don't be afraid, refill the glass;
Escape the prison of your reasons.
To forget the sorrow of a grieving mother:
Kiss a woman; that brings up joy.

15

I am lost in the shadows past yesterday;
And I am faint of looming tomorrow.
My glass is empty, butler, pour me another;
I can't grasp this short dream.

16

A rosy red lip like wine in a glass,
I love them for the taste of their wine.
If her figure was not shaped like a wine-flask
No doubt, I would not embrace her.

RAFIQ SABIR

Dr Rafiq Sabir (1950 – present) joined the Kurdish resistance movement in the early 1980s after having been pressured by Saddam Hussein's regime. After the destruction of villages and the *Anfal* campaign of mass killings by the Iraqi Baath regime, Sabir left for Sweden in 1989 where he continues to reside to this day.

His first collection was published in 1974; between then and 2006 eleven of his collections were put to print. In 2014, his entire collection was released in Kurdistan.

The first time I met Sabir was in Baghdad during the 1970s, when he worked as a journalist. I met him again in 1982, in a no-man's land on the Iraq-Iran border, associated with the communist party, fighting against Saddam Hussein's regime. I met him more frequently after I moved to Europe.

Silence

Your silence is a continuous journey,
Between doubts and certainties.

Your silence is like the silence of sunlight,
It is a contemporary means of communication.

In the climax of silence and surprise,
You are as colourful as a spring day.

You are happy and enthralling,
Like the blossom of a new day.

This form of expression becomes you;
Silent words from you are precious.

I love your silence,
I love your uniqueness,
I love your mysteries,
When they dance like spring flowers.

I love your eyes when
They reveal your depths to me.

Self-knowledge

You gave silence a voice.
In the path of sunlight,
You made me follow you.

In the infinite, you showed me finite,

In words,
You introduced me to creation.
In echoes of silence,
You made me familiar
To myself.

With You

I wake up to the floral scent of your body;
I still don't know where I am.
I close my eyelids
And yet I am watching.
Your body a book of sunlight,
Your clear silhouette an eternal mirror.

I am neither awake nor ready.
As always with you,
It is as if time neither passes nor stands still.

Sanctuary

The night, like me, is wide awake,
And you, like a child, dressed up in the other room.
Outside, nothing is visible,
Except for fear.
Inside, I am immersed in the resonance of silence;
Quivering,
As the stem of a poppy sways under heavy rain.

In your sleepy embrace,
Warm me up,
Or hide my body and soul
In your hands.

Together

We have only each other.
We have leaned towards one another for so long,
Our bodies share the same scent,
The same sweet smell of rain and moonlight.

Just like two embers,
We lean towards the cold,
As we play with sunlight.
We lean towards dreams and loneliness;
And we play with life and impossibilities.

We have no one except each other.
Together, we establish:
A country with dreams,

A home of light,
And a future with love.

I was not Lonely

I was not lonely;
The night was a corpse that lay next to me.
The time was fog and tears.
The homeland was a handful of dust in the wind,
Intertwined with my soul.

I was not lonely;
I was set afire by secrecy;
I was a book, read by the depth of the sea.

Intertwine

Do you know where we are?
How far have we gone?
And what we are flying towards?
Do you know where love
Has taken us?

We have given our souls to each other.
I never ask:
Where you have been?
Where do you go?
Wherever you are
It is normal.
Whatever distance is between us both,
You are still close to me.

What is distance anyhow?

If you are not with me in person,
With whomever else you may be,
It does not matter.
As long as you are happy,
I can survive.
What is a body?
Our souls are forever
Intertwined.

In the Rain

Your shadow is lying down in the rain;
You read the words of thunder.
The rain washes the body of darkness.
The night is a mirror.
Your appearance is wet with fear,
And a secret is brightening it up.
In your hands,
A star is asleep.

It was Morning Just Like Now

It was morning just like now;
The most beautiful time for being lost:
You are waiting for me;
I am looking for nothing.

It was morning just like now:
Neither sunny nor shady;

Neither silent nor talking;
Neither the end nor the start was clear;
Only an open road and
Two shattered bodies;
Two shadows shining;
On the other side of time.

Behind time,
I was waiting for vagueness.
I was guided just like the blind.
My hands were empty:
Full of doubt and fear;
Full of endlessness;
In the far end of the space, you disappeared.
Time stopped.
It was morning just like now.

Freedom

I look for my freedom;
And my hands wake up by touching your body.

You are the substance of things;
The space of dreams and place of soul-worship.
Your body yields to shining flowers;
Your hands reflect the future to me;
Just like a mirror.

Your shine is an eternal worshipping focus,
Being a prisoner within you is my freedom.

With What Shall I Depict You?

With what shall I depict you?
With the horizon of rain;
With thirst;
With tiredness;
With dreams;
Or with the forest?

With what shall I depict you?
With a flock of sunrays;
With a country drawn in blood;
With songs;
With breathing;
With an avalanche;

Or with a flood?

You look like existence itself; with what shall I not depict you?
You look like non-existence; with what shall I depict you?

Selection

Do you remember, how you ended up in this town,
Where the fog of time covered everything,
Except for a glimmer of hope.
A big dream followed by grand labour,
That may take you to the shores of insanity.

You look at yourself and the surroundings,
Life looks for further openings.
Your surroundings look for loneliness;
And the passing days for waiting.

Do you think
Beauty has arrived here?
The words ring the bell of truth;
And the truth is the path to freedom.

Freedom is the willingness to be free and have a choice.
It is possible that loneliness is the split road
Towards wondering or self-knowledge.

Life could be an unclimbed mountain
For climbing or flying away.

Parallel

1

You are lying down next to me;
Your body is pure white, covered with fog.
Your face is sleepy.
We are like two riverbanks facing each other.
The night is the river between us.
We are two parallel lines.
The space between us justifies our existence.

2

You are lying down next to me;
A secret is shining in your eyes.
I am not here and looking far away
To the depth of space,
To the past, the mirror of the present,
To the distance between us.
I read the darkness.
I communicate silently with your body,
With myself.
Like a diverted wave
Exhausted, I'm moving towards your shore.

3

Behind your body,
I see the space.
The fading borders between being and not being.
Behind your looks,
I see certainty and uncertainty.

4

I am lying down like a body still next to you.
It is calm and alienation is remote.
The night is like an undertaker;
And silence is the graveyard's caretaker.

5

You are like the sunlight:
I cannot touch you;
Or like darkness;
I cannot escape from you.

6

I am lying next to you,
Your forehead in resting is blossoming.
Your breasts in the darkness
Shine like two stars.
Your breath warming up the night,
Your looks sometimes shatter me,
And others provide me with life,
They light up the time.

7

How could I free myself from you?
While like two parallel lines,
The space between us reflects the signs of our existence.
How could I touch you?
While we are two facing riverbanks,
The sunlight is the river between us.

To Loneliness

To be enamoured with freedom, lonely times.
It is a bridge between light and darkness;
Or it is the sparkle of time and place, loneliness.

The roads are exposed; the night wears moonlight;
And I walk into the loneliness.
A dark forest is on my way,
The moon stares at me,
And the horizon awaits me.

In the clear mirror of loneliness, I see myself.
I am a truth mixed with doubts.

My body is a blue ink dot tattooed into the darkness;
My soul is a drop in the sea of time.

As if fate has gone ahead of me.
Amongst this loneliness, I move towards myself.
The night stares at me.
It is not with me, it whispers to itself.
It is not with me, it sings lonely songs;
And yet loneliness reads me.
I am in its presence, a little bit of sunlight;
And the night with my reflection is brightened up.

I am a drop in the sea of time,
A fact mixed with doubt.

GORAN MERIWANI

Goran Meriwani (1955 - present), my older brother, was an active Kurdish poet during the 1970s. Meriwani was born in Sulaymaniyah and left to live in exile in the late 1970s. After fleeing the Baath regime for political reasons, he only wrote in the privacy of his home, not submitting his work for publication. For a long while he halted his public activities, such as openly reciting or publishing his poetry. He was very influential in the 1970s, especially amongst his own generation. Meriwani resumed writing poetry publicly in the last few years and is sharing his pieces on social media networks. A fresh and unique poetic style can now be attributed to him.

From an early age, it had been clear that he had a good command over the art of poetry. He could write clearly, using a vocabulary from different eras of time and from wide range of Kurdish dialects. Meriwani writes when the words come to him, no matter how irregularly that occurs, and when the muse hits him, he offers his own refreshing perspective to the reader. His vast knowledge of Kurdish classical poetry gave Meriwani his competitive edge; he believed that this was a crucial component to being a good contemporary poet.

Although he does not publish his classical work, his private circle is very familiar with the entire body of his poetry, his depiction of classical Kurdish poems, his own classical expression and style, and his beautiful use of vocabulary and rhythm (*Arud*). His knowledge of several languages, including Kurdish, Arabic, Farsi, English and Swedish, has helped shape his own poetic expression.

Meriwani's regional experience and international knowledge of poetry have given him an extraordinary point of view. Although there are no similarities with other Kurdish poets in Meriwani's work, recently with access to his poetry through social media networks, numerous writers are inspired by his poetic voice which is reflected in their writings. He does not write in a lyrical format, but he gives inner rhymes to his poetry. The strong unity of his subjects makes the reader to forget the other aspects of poetry. He does not keep it quite; he informs that he moves away from all known poetic metering. Once I read one of his poems to inform that there is not known rhythm to his poem. He replied that it is based on sounds of waves mixed with a Kurdish classic song, which he named.

His recent poetry deals with the inner emotions of human beings. Meriwani can be very critical but in an indirect and gentle fashion. When he is critical of extrajudicial killings in Kurdistan, he does not directly criticise the political regime; rather he praises the victims and links them to concepts such as justice and beauty. This is clear, for example, in a few verses of the poem *You, are not coming home!*, *Kobane*, *He will also be departing*, *I am departing*, *Afrin* and *I am not in Kobane*. Although these are examples of local injustices, Meriwani turns them to global issues by shifting the focus from the political system to the victim.

The vocabulary that Meriwani uses is not unfamiliar to us and it consists of simple things and phenomena around us, and yet he builds sophisticated narratives around a subject to deliver his views in a crystal-clear fashion. Examples of the vocabulary he uses are rain, garden, home, winter, the cold, fathers, mothers, war, flowers, his homeland, rooms, stones, stars, home, spring, us, you, neighbours, love, trees, etc.

You Are not Coming Home!

Dedicated to my late older brother, Dilshad Meriwani, who arrested and disappeared forever by the Baath regime. (GM)

When the rain drizzles down,
When the green leaves are about to turn yellow,
When the pain of grief for you is unbearable,
At night, clouds are intimate,
To give birth to snowflakes and drops of rain.
I open the door;
To find only blizzards.
You are not coming home again!

When widespread bitterly cold frost arrives,
The heart of The Göta älv in front of our home

Stops beating, suffering from the cold,
A black cloud
Blocks the view of my sky.
In my loneliness and with no one around me,
I catch a shiver for being far away.
I open the door for you;
I merely see snow, white snow.
You are not coming home again!

When in Summer, the heat chases away the cold;
In the shade of our apple tree,
Dylan asks me about you:[27]
Which type of human was he?
What sort of music and songs did he love?
He will be back in a moment, I tell him;
Go and open the door; he will be there!
To see you with a bag of broken-up sorrow
And a bunch of stunning poetry.
But you are not coming home again!

During spring,
When towering plants blossom;
The sky occasionally with a breeze
Wipes away a drop of dew.
Our home echoes birds and sparrows chirping and singing.
My heart would ask with a sigh, "Will I see you again?"

Days would pass to welcome fresh days ahead.
And the time,
In front of our gate,

---

[27] Dylan is Goran Meriwani's son.

Is stuck in its past.
I tell Dylan,
This time, I smell the scent of a visitor;
We both love.
I open the door for you;
I only feel the scent of spring.
You are not coming home again!

Burning

Dedicated to environmental campaigners who died in
fighting forest fire in the Mariwan region, Kurdistan Region,
Iran, on Saturday, August 25th 2018. Mohammad Pjuyi,

Sharif Bajwar, Omed Koneposhi and Rahmat Hakimi-Nia
died fighting the spreading of the fire. (GM)

What a gloomy time!
The sun moves her head sideways to carry the coffin of
Light.
The sea sighs;
The sky gently wipes away her tears;
The shore submerges in tears;
The fish shoal in groups;
The shark's mouth is an unnamed cemetery;
And I am sitting by the sea, whose full-of-trouble head rests
on my lap.
The sun is merely a foot away; she is soaked in blood.
The sea, the sun and I, all three of us,
Carry a bleak day on our shoulders,
As if the earth, or our hearts, have lost a war.
What a gloomy time!
The smoke of my breath smells like fire, as if it was the End
of humanity.

Next Time

Next time, when we decide,
We move to live on a star;
I am simply bored on earth.

In our neighbourhood,
No one likes the scent of flowers;
No one thinks the voice of cuckoos is sweet;
No one looks at the sky; and,

No one finds the stars attractive.

Next time, when we are ready,
We move to live on a star;
And, if you move in with me,
I shall never come back;
I shall not be back to
Neighbourhoods or towns on earth.

War

Those who know each other,
Send those who do not know each other,
To kill one another.

When the dust of gunpowder settles,
Those who know each other,
Gather around huge feasts,
In magnificent castles
To settle scores.

And those who do not know each other,
Hopelessly move around on battle grounds
Searching for corpses.

Afrin

You portray a forest that just began to blossom,
With no clouds over her head.
Deep inside you, a spring or a stream flows.

You appear as a forest that has raised her head recently;
In every leaf, you have hidden secrets of a light.

You depict a forest; during evenings, I get lost in it.
Unintentionally, every single part of my body wears your colours.
Just like my mother,
You have submerged your colours in my soul.

You imagine a forest without trees
Without a name,
And without a forest,
You have no trees.

And I image a sapling tree;
Without you,
I even doubt my green dreams.

Winter

This poem arose from a discussion with my brother Rebwar Fatah. (GM)
Suddenly winter has arrived;
With her marching white soldiers,
Conquered the homeland.
Hållingsjö is frozen;
And lost all her power to shiver.

The trees are holding their breath,
As if they grew in front of gun barrels.
Their hands turned numb,

They cannot even reply to my greetings.

A hawk with a broken wing,
Left on his own.
He and I stroll together in the morning,
But we are not sure,
Which one of us
Will outlast this winter.

He Will also be Departing

Dedicated to Dr Hoshyar Esmayil

Dr Hoshyar Esmayil was a religious man and the prayer leader of a local mosque in Erbil, the Kurdistan Region of Iraq. He was also an outspoken campaigner against corruption and injustice in Kurdistan. On November 22nd 2016, he was shot in front of his home in Erbil, and lost his life in the local hospital. No one claimed responsibility for the murder and the Kurdistan authorities never investigated it seriously. He was not an isolated case, rather one amongst a series of assassination campaigns dated from 1991, since the establishment of Kurdish self-rule in Kurdistan. The victims have all raised their voices against the corruption and injustice of Kurdistan's authorities. These murders have not been investigated seriously. Goran Meriwani wrote this short poem after the murder of Dr Hoshyar Esmayil.

He will also be departing;
Opening the front door of his home,
To say goodbye.
A bullet pierces his chest.
Yet, instead of blood,

His wound bleeds justice.

He will also be departing;
To see justice,
Before being present in front of God's throne.

He will also be departing;
To leave behind a bullet shell and four children;
With a country populated
With fake representatives on the throne of God.

He will also be departing;
As he is leaving,
I open the upper buttons of my shirt,
Awaiting for someone to knock on my door.

I am departing

Dedicated to Widad Dhokyy

Widad Hussein, known as Widad Duhoky, was assassinated, on August 13th 2016, between the city of Duhok and the town of Smul, in Iraqi Kurdistan. This region is under the control of Masoud Barzani's group, KDP. Widad was kidnapped by two vehicles and his body was dumped in the village of Sejeyy. He was 28 years of age. He was working for a pro-PKK website. The extrajudicial killing, same as all the others in Kurdistan, was never investigated by the Kurdistan authorities. At the time, Widad's brother told media outlets that from the day that Widad started working for pro-PKK media until his murder, he was called to the KDP security offices 11 times. This is one of many unresolved extrajudicial killings in Kurdistan.

1

I am departing
To lie down next to a river,
In the fields,
To be full of stars at night,
And during the day,
To be full of tiny waves of light
And occasionally,
Gushing water and fountains of sadness.

2

I am departing,
To grow next to a tree;
Just like her, I produce branches;
Grow roots
And talk like her.
When my heart is full of homesickness;
Leaf after leaf, during autumnal days,
I fall down.

3

I am departing,
To tell an ant,
I am tired,
Hoping to allow me to sleep next to her babies;
And I promise;
Not to reveal their colony.
And even if I die of hunger,
I would not touch their wealth.

4

I am departing,
To a faraway place.
I climb up a mountain;
To tell her peak,
Clear the way!
I stand in your place.
I look all around myself;
I fill my heart with big rocks,
And my soul with nests of sacred light.
A morning, after 29 years
Of dry springs,
I happily unite
With a cloud.

5

I am departing,
To lay down next to Nona,
To ask,
Are we repairing our arc?
You have to make me one promise;
With all other living beings,
Only
Have a Widad on board.

6

I do not know, where to go!
Where to hide myself!
In the end,
A bullet comes;
From no side,
Out of nowhere,

Only,
To hit my heart.

My friends, I think,
This time,
It is going to kill me.

Myself

I cross street after street;
Wandering around the squares;
Looking for you,
I do not find you.

I search the woods;

Look at the tree branches.
When a bird flies by,
I extend wings to fly with her.
I look in every town,
Cross village after village for you.

When a butterfly lands,
I smell the scent of her neck,
I do not sense you.

A flower, a drop of rain,
Or a ray of light,
Are all blended with your memories;
Just like bees pour honey
Into my inner roots.

No place is left,
Where I haven't looked for you.
There is not a messenger or post-rider,
I have not asked about your traces.
A passer-by,
I have described your complexion
And yet there is no sign of you

An early morning,
I wake up;
When I see your image
In the mirror opposite me,
Without your sunset-like colours
How could I recognise you.
After 37 years of being exiled!

My Father

I told him,
When I am back,
I bring an armful of love,
And a tiny drop of faithfulness.

I told him,
When we meet again,
We talk about being far away from each other.
You talk about fatherhood,
And I talk about faithfulness.
You talk about silence,
And I talk about echoes.

I told him,
Beyond faithfulness,
I have no interest in love.

When we sit together,
In our garden,
Upon my return,
You talk about Zrebar and Mariwan[28]
I talk about a Swedish pheasant,[29]
A Norwegian kingfisher,
A Finnish wild pigeon.

---

[28] Meriwan is a Kurdish region in Kurdistan-Iran where Meriwani's father was born before moving to Kurdistan-Iraq. Zrebar is a beautiful lake near the city of Meriwan (aka: Mariwan or Marivan).

[29] Goran Meriwani has been living in Sweden, his exile homeland, since the late 1970s.

We laugh loudly;
We take off the skins of sadness,
And wipe a tiny bit for being far away from each other,
With a green leaf of father and son.
Just like a partridge,
In a refugee camp,
As he chirps, he expresses the sentiment of being exiled,
And we talk.

I told him,
All the roads end up unified;
All the views end up in
Seeing.

And the few birds in the sky
Are signs of a chase and silence;
The empty forests are
Victims of hunters;
Only faithfulness
Takes us back to the lovers.

He said,
Leaving is easy;
Coming back is tough.

Taking the first step on the way
Is the sign of loving life.

The roads and alleys of life
Are not only bright and dark,
Human sufferings are sophisticated
And are not single-sided.

I told him,
I do not know.
I am still a child.

Wherever you go,
I come with you.
A grave, a shrine, are not an obstacle.
You taught me to think.
I miss you so much;
Now I am a refugee,
Escaped from life.

I Am Moving Away from This Place

I move away from this place;
I move away from earth;
I move towards the sky,
And ask a star
To shelter me,
For the rest of my life.
I shall become a neighbour
Of the moon, the sun,
And some beautiful creatures.

I move away from this place,
Moving towards the sky.
In the morning,
In a car made out of a cloud,
I embark on a safari
I may visit the dusk orchards,

Pick a yellow apple
To taste it to my full liking
Or in the evening
Silently,
Fully naked,
In the silence of the horizon,
Swim for a while.

I am moving away from this place:
I shall not be the familiar 'Goran'
And on my way back home,
It is possible that I give a lift to
A grieving owl;
A Water Strider deprived of springs
A lame ladybird
A disabled swallow victimised by war
To exchange love
Until we become the guest of mortality.

I move away from this place;
I move towards the sky;
Far away from the sounds of bombs and planes,
Rivers hanged with their legs.
Myself and I move around together in the sky.
I visit the home of this or that star
To tell them the narratives of war.
I tell them,
How we are exterminated
In the name of God.
I tell them how the firefly
Lost her vision in the war,
Or the foal whose beauty

Was violated in a prison.
I write your stories one after another,
Daily across the stars.

I am heartbroken here.
I move away and do not stay.
Earth for you,
And sky for me.
Weapons for you,
And disabilities resulting out of wars for me.
The slander of big books for you.
Doubt reaching my bones for me.
Victory for you;
Thinking of being and not being;
Of a beautiful creature
Only for me,
But
Now I am moving away.
I don't wish to see,
Anyone of you, not even in the sky.

We

We were playing
All day long;
And during the night,
We watched the stars.

My father was planting flowers,
Counting the pomegranates
Of our garden.

My mother was concerned
About us being cold.

Suddenly the war arrived
Killed my older brother
And we were dispersed.

From that date onwards,
We have neither played;
Nor seen stars;
Not even tasted
The drying pomegranates
Of our garden, ever Again.

Biography of a Kurdish Family

Your father was a Peshmerga;[30]
Who did not return from a battlefield.
You mother wore a black dress, mourning for him;
And laid her head down in sorrow.
Your older brother is unemployed;
He has to take part in a battlefront.

As for yourself,
I am embarrassed to predict your future;

As for myself,
_____

---

[30] Peshmerga is a Kurdish word and a name given to a Kurdish freedom fighter. It literally means 'ahead of death', i.e. the people who put death in front of them. It usually refers to an armed rebel.

What else is left to do?

As for the politicians,
They are not ashamed;
Neither by our past,
Nor by our future.

My Mother

I was a child;
I was running after the rain;
I was curious to know where its home is.

Gently running after snow
To know how she melts,
With graceful white hair.

I waited for hail;
When she arrived,
I followed her steps.
I wished to know,
What would open her ice-cold heart.

I was a child;
Impressed with the sky;
How does she tie the knot of a rainbow
With only one hand?
Why does she wrap
A scarf of clouds around her neck
And cover herself?
For whom are her blue eyes

Burning?

I was a child;
Resting calmly on your laps;
You looked at me with deep love.

My room was full of hail, thunder and rain;
Full of clouds, moon and a piece of the sky.
Those who were born to destitution and without mothers,
At night,
Stayed with me.

I was a child,
You made me,
The king of my room.
Before I sleep,
You asked me,
To place a hope in my heart
As if I had the discovery of secrets this world and the other
The day after I was made speechless by fear.

I was a child;
I do not know,
Why I grew up,
This fast
And for what purpose!

When I Am Not in Kobane

Kobane would not fall tonight.
I try to sleep.

I keep her in my heart and hands,
Fearing that she'll get stolen.

I am embarrassed tonight
To not be in Kobane,
To not fight alongside
Jani, Leylan and Matson.[31]
To not talk to the Islamic State with fire.
To not have bread and tea with them;
And count their bullets from time to time.

Tonight will also pass.
Kobane will fight on her feet.
Tonight, the darkness gives away the brightness.
Kobani will not be defeated
Even with the Gods of enemies.

Tonight, I wipe off the shameful sweat of
Shangal and Jalawla,[32]
With the blood of Kobane.

Tonight, I will die one hundred times
Of shame,
For being far away from Kobane.

---

31 These are names of female fighters in Kobane. Kobane is a Kurdish city in
northern Syria, which is a part of a Kurdish political entity known as Rojava. It is
well-known for its women fighters. Kobane was the first city that resisted the
Islamic State group. It became the symbol of resistance.

32 These two towns are in Iraqi Kurdistan, which were defeated by Islamic State
fighters without much resistance. The KDP forces, led by Massoud Barzani, simply
left Shangal for the Islamic State, leading to a mass killing of the Yezidi Kurds.

Kobane is Alone

Kobane is alone
In fighting, in death;
In the evening stroll across the trenches; and,
Under the loud, rippling sound of gunfire.

She is alone;
Under God's injustice,
In the sound of the final gunshot,
In untimed and impatient death.

She is courageous,
Her pure hatred,
Like gunshots of uprising are full of sacred light;
Death, like love for the enemy,
Is far from her.

In the battles, she is lonely.
In death, she is lonely.
Under the cruel sky,
She is without support and shelter;
But in the hearts of you and I,
My mother, my father and my children,
She is all Kurds.

MOHAMMED OMAR OSMAN

Mohammed Omar Osman (1957 - present) is known as the 'autumn General' as most of his poems address seasonal aspects. In one poem, he even claims to be the 'autumn General'. He asserts that no other poet has seen autumn as he has. These poems are extracts from his published collections known *as Le Ghurbata* or 'In Exile'. The first edition was published in 2002 and the second one in 2012.

Osman has not written a large collection of poems and yet he is a very well-known Kurdish poet of his generation. He affirmed that volume does not determine a poet. His poetic vocabulary is characterised by autumnal themes such as leaves, rain, storm, death, grave, sadness and depression.

As children, we used to spend a good part of our summer holidays together. Osman's family's store was next to ours and it was expected of boys to help their fathers during summer holidays. My older brother Goran Meriwani, Osman and I used to meet in the shopping complex to play together.

In Exile

In my depressed heart, a cloud cries;
That does not rain through my eyes.
My life is snow, spread in the sun;
Merely chasing its own death.[33]

Who would put the autumnal bursts of my exiled heart
On the laps of a red spring?
It is a lost ship in a troubled sea.
Will it arrive at the shore one day?

I should not deceive myself, my isolated self;
My shore is made of storms and heavy rains.
No one would cry over my shoulder;
Only fog clamours through the evening.

For happiness, life is too short;
For misery, it never ends.
It's iafire set to mpossible, snow in the sun!

---

[33] This is a translated extract of a long poem.

It disintegrates after a short while!

What is the beauty of snow in the sun:
If it does not make the dusk bleed;
If it does not turn to jangles of cries;
As its life melts at its own peril?

Oh, how much I wish to cry;
To dissolve my heart in tears?
I am lonely, lonely; and no one embraces
This pain of mine.

In the grasp of loneliness, last night;
I went to pet a distressed dog.
The colour of his eyes resembled autumnal leaves;
He left me too; how unfortunate.

During a midnight stroll,
A dog became familiar with my walking path.
I was staring at his yellow eyes;
He poured streams of compassion at my feet.

In the grasp of hunger, how sad!
That dog may now have passed away.
When he takes his last breath,
Would he think of my loneliness again?

The flowers of a few clouds now forming a bunch;
And a thunder has become its vase.
The vase breaks and with one moment
Soaks my body, the showery rain.

Under a roof where I am waiting;
Rain flows down and makes me shiver;
It reminds me of the past days;
Her looks were ember in my bright blood.

It reminds me of those days;
My heart was ice-cold, my vision set in the sun.
Drugs were unfamiliar to my blood;
I had neither hot tears, nor agony in my heart.

We departed without goodbyes;
My dreams went up in fog and smoke.
The heart in ruins, a nest of crows;
My grief: a song for nightingales.

I shall become a Sufi, living in a desert;
Dreaming of God's face and wonder:
Whether he would hide me in his sacred light;
And listen to the echoes of my intense grief!

I shall convert to a monk, waiting in a church;
When the bells begin to toll, grieve over
My dressed-up figure in total black
And that of the calm and quiet crucifixion of Jesus.

In the church, place of my emotions and tears,
A light-eyed nun covered in black:
One by one lights up the candles;
And embraces my frozen heart.

For a minute, I seek shelter under an umbrella;
I remember her classical face.

When the clouds clear,
She will disappear like drops of rain.

I wish, I could in just one glass
Collect and drink all these clouds;
And climb up a thunder-ladder
To reach up and wash my heart with fire.

During evenings, my head becomes ash;
In the shadows of a love tree
My cry tree is barren with no branches;
Who would share with her some flowers of smiles?

People took me for a madman;
Sighing for the days, I was under the rain;
My heart full of tears was melting,
Awaiting her during the evening.

People took me for a madman;
They do not know, I can read the 'winds';
Drops of rain are my poetry words;
The fire of love mixed my blood.

I wish I could set myself on fire;
My smoke becomes a veil over your face;
Or die and dogs eat my flesh;
My vision: a prison between death and a coffin.

A Telegraph

Do you know why my stormy world of poetry is always set in autumn?
I have nothing more than autumn;
autumn is my homeland.

I have exiled myself;
Do not ask me what it is like to be in exile.
I am displaced, lonely and dispersed. That is my life.

I wish to be a cloud to pour rain over your tall figure;
I wish to be a butterfly turning into soot;
When, late at night, it flies into the flame of your lamp.

We are like two drops of dew;
Tomorrow, the unfortunate sun will burn them off;
Or we are two leaves;
The autumnal wind takes in the lap of the unknown!

Being Lost

The cloud burns and stutters inhalation; the night is late.
The drops of rain, the falling leaves of a crying season,
Of a faraway silent forest;
The drops of rain, like thousands of soft fingers and hands,
Knock on the cold glass of my room's window;
When I raised my head, the streams of rain turned into thick blood.

Through the streams of rainy blood, I look at faraway lands;
A shadow moves fast towards the graveyard, passes quickly;

I recognise the wet shadow in the night rain;
A mad poet, whose figure sank into the sorrow and fog.

Occasionally thunder and lightning
Brighten the path where he walks;
The thunder is the only night lamp.

What is he up to? What is he doing tonight?
Who shall he bury in a confined grave?
Why has he no spade and pickaxe on his shoulder?
Where is the deceased? Where is the coffin? Where are the
mourners?
He is the gravedigger and the decedent, too.
He is the funeral and the mourner, too.

Without anyone knowing the reason; no one knows, no one;
With the burial of his father's body;
Came the burial of the poetry collection book;
Bubbling and burbles were cut from the waterfalls and
steams;
Just like an alien bird is held within a cage.

The poems written with the ink of a melting heart;
Rivers with their tears;[34]
Why did they not protest
To rip the confined grave wide open?

He is stepping continuously;
Every so often a voice is heard that whispers:

---

34 The poet names two rivers, Tanjaro and Zalim, which are situated in the
Sulaymaniyah province, Kurdistan.

138

You are not a devil; how do you open your father's grave?
Why do you open the windows of sin
Over the room of your ice-cold soul!

Autumnal Night

Tonight, the inhabitants of the town have closed their
windows tight;
Except for me, my window is wide open.
Who is, like me, filling his glass with sorrows of yellow
autumnal leaves?
I am just about to shed my blood over a bare tree.

The boughs and twigs have turned into thousands of
worshipping hands;
The wind has carried millions of martyred leaves on its back.
Sadly, the leaves are being trampled over;
They are bewildered in the earth and dust.

Tonight, the leaves are dead butterflies;
Not visiting lamps or candle fire.
Tonight, the leaves are mummy fish;
Not uniting with streams and rivers.

Every so often a wave of memories
Takes me back to the old tree;
Which, like me, was an offspring of autumn.
The old tree that in early days
Was a rare hideout for my lover and me.

The old tree that I once thought,

Even if the black wind confiscated its last leaf,
The hand of every bare bough and twig
Would lock in her embrace hundreds of our whispering
flowers.

I wish I could free all these leaves
From the claws of cold midnight winds;
With the threads of a beautiful rainbow, I sew their coffins
In a graveyard, I hand them over to a night angel.

The night lay down and the magic of autumn,
Led my ice-cold head out of the window.
I even feel sorrow for the lonely dogs in the rain;
There are not only one or two and I'll lend them my own
clothes.

Grieving

What a doomed, depressing day!
As the sun chokes in the heavy fog.
A poet is in the coffin of the sun;
Crying, and winter is attacking him.

The fire of the chest turned to ashes;
My ruined heart is deadly cold now;
How I disappeared in winter!
I used to be full of fire and flames.

Where did the days go where her looks,
Like autumnal leaves, fell over my numbed body?
To a diseased man like me, two gardens of her eyes

Offer leaves of tears as a present.

Why don't our heartbeats flow into one another?
The hand of winter is about to knock on the door.
O, I shall collapse in a corner;
I die quietly, a destitute man's death.

Before we departed,
I did not say; I was submerged in shivers and snow.
Imagination led me towards warmer lands;
The snow became my own place and shelter.

When I was with her, snow was ember;
Even when leaves were absent from the trees,
I could imagine a flower garden
On the bare branches covered in snow.

Snow to me is a funeral suit,
That's forced me into suffering.
In my lover's memory, I stand in the way.
I seek shelter under the cloud's wings.

I cry with the clouds, remembering
The days that would never come back.
The snow that fell since her departure,
How it would melt in my own heart!

Who would hide me from this storm?
Who would be an umbrella over my head?
I don't see anyone who has her looks,
To request her mercy, just before I die.

The snowflakes on her evening departure,
All become flocks of black crows.
In a world that is full of black umbrellas;
I should not turn snow into an umbrella.

Snow was a coffin, a white coffin.
My lover rested her head in it.
Just overnight my head turned white,
Even with my sighs, snow did not melt.

I cried for a while and fell on my knees,
To pour my tears on her footprints;
I did not wish to wipe them out,
Crying over them till early dawn.

I wish I could rip my heart out;
To pour its blood on her footprints;
A row of red footprints over the snow;
No beauty could ever match it.

I begged my God, what would happen
If the sun never rose again?
So her footprints remain on the snow,
Forever and ever!

O I had not known, that her footprints
Were the last glimmer of my hope;
Wiped out under people's footsteps.
They are all young victims at the hands of death.

No one would even know that they were her footprints;
Or that it was my heart under the steps,

.

That would turn to water and fall under the
Snowfalls of the evening?

And now, despite the autumn of life
Taking me towards my grave, its cold breeze and fog
In my eyes, a cloud of pain and anguish,
Thunders bursting with its sorrow.

Although after her, I search for a dusk,
To hand me over the fogs of doom.
For many days, I wandered around;
My heart broke and I shed so many tears.

An omen's hand hasn't knocked on my door;
I saw no one to surprise my heart,
To annihilate the winter of my room;
And to bury the shadows of my loneliness.

I am not sure if she will be back,
Before a grave takes my body into a dark embrace;
And she washes me out in her tears;
Ashes of my heart start fires of my love
Over her body, all over again.

VENUS FAIQ

Venus Faiq, born in Sulaymaniyah, is a female poet and journalist who lived in exile in the Netherlands. Since she returned to Kurdistan, she worked in journalism and writing. She has written poetry in both Kurdish and Arabic. Her first collection of poetry, entitled *Gunahe jiwanekan* or "The Fine Sins", was published in 2001. She contributed two poems to this anthology, which were handed over to me by her personally.

Fading

You should have arrived much earlier,
Before history began,
Before dreaming began.

You should have arrived much earlier:
In order to know you,
In order to introduce you,
To the dawn of my life,
To my mother.
To my childhood friends.

You should have arrived much earlier:
Before love began,
Before the apple ripened,
Before Adam's expulsion from Eden.

You should have arrived much earlier:
Before my lifetime grew,
Much longer than the road
That leads back to the beginning
Before the season of farewell began;
Before the season of sorrow and separation;
Before the season of crying and isolation.

You should have arrived much earlier:
Before leaving the nearby tribes behind
To be burned alive;
Before learning any lessons from the girls
I saw being violated.

You know! Your arrival now is nonsense!
What is the point of arriving
After the beginning?
After the event?

Now, it is too late!
You pass by my voice,
And you don't hear the sound:
Of the fragmentations;
Of my suns and moons.
You don't understand the years that incised me.

You pass by my breathing,
And you don't notice the dulling of my bright eyes,
The fading of my waiting puzzles you.

When you arrived,
History opened its vexed arms.
And then you were just like the breathing of a stone,
Which lay below the waterfalls:
Dreaming of mist, cotton and red roses,
Dreaming of Cleopatra's lips.

Now, at this late time:
What do you have to say?
How much do you understand of the gloom of my fate?
What do you understand of a vain and yet yielding woman?
What do you understand of a proud and yet alienable
woman?
Whose tender days, weeks and months have long passed,
Left with only years of decay.

Why have you not arrived:
Before aging;
Before fading;
The times when we were breathing, just like the water;
And thinking just like the fish?

Why couldn't you arrive:
Before the event;
Before history opened the gates of travel;
Before my exiled hair grew white;
Before the ending began?
You should have come much earlier!

Darwish

Like the rain falling on my soft body,
It shatters me and leaves no opportunity,
To gather my broken pieces.
Like the rain showering upon me,
It leaves me breathless;
And does not forgive my eyes,
When they grow sleepy.

He enjoys making me angry,
Invading my heart
And then making it up to me.

With the perfume that spills over the brightness of my eyes,
He washes, not to pray, but to become drunk.
He prays in front of God's gate,
He challenges me, "You are a part of me and born of me

Otherwise, set a limit to my kisses.
I am you and you are born of me;
Otherwise, set a limit to my sins."

With the dew that spills over my lips,
He cleanses his sins.
He becomes angry with me,
Leaves me behind,
Takes an oath and comes back to me,
But he does not have it his way.

He opens the gate of his chest for my fingers to swim in,
Then opens his heart to martyr me.

Like the rain falling on my soft body,
Shatters me and does not allow me to gather my fractured
pieces.
Like the rain showering upon me does not forgive my eyes,
If they grew sleepy.

Dilsoz Hama

Dilsoz Abdulrahman Hama, known as Dilsoz Hama (circa 1970 – present) was born in a refugee camp in the Kurdistan region of Iran. Her exact date of birth was never recorded. Dilsoz Hama attended school in Sulaymaniyah and graduated in 1993 from the University of Mosul.

She started her political activism and writings early in her life. She was wounded during the civil unrest against the Baath regime in 1982 in her hometown. Her first short story was published in

1984. Dilsoz Hama has been living in the Netherlands since 1998. She has published two collections, *"He requests my hand in autumn"* and *"The only lover"*. She is an active writer.

Dilsoz Hama started to take writing more seriously in the early 1990s as her work was published in local Kurdish publications. She believes that she did not write much in the early 2000s. As she reached a new period in her life, poetry became her fate. Dilsoz Hama is influenced by Iranian, Arabic, and Latin American poetry.

The first time I met Disoz was in Sulaymaniyah, Kurdistan. When she moved to Europe, we kept in touch and we met a few times.

Snapshots of womanhood

1
The most unproductive journey,
The most hopeless tour,
Have been the love trips.
It was the search for a Farhad.[35]
How did I escape a fate,
That was written in my palm lines,
And on my forehead?

2
My lover, oh my lover!
Once a month he sends me a letter.
Yet it fills up all the 30 days with sunlight.
And all 30 nights with stars.

---

35 Farhad is the lover of Shirin in a Kurdish love story similar to Romeo and Juliet.

Once a season he phones.
Yet it fills up all my three months with songs,
Roars of rivers and whisperings of winds.

Once a year I see him.
Once a year his fishes flow into my blood vessels.
Once a year his birds land on my waist
And my kisses reach his figure.
Yet, for eternity, my feeling is pregnant,
Making me wait for the rest of the year,
Or even for the rest of my life.

3
The mirror during the journey of my gaze says, you are
beautiful.
Loneliness, throughout my life told me, it is useless.

4
At home,
I don't wear a bra,
I walk around barefoot.
That is why when I am just about to open the front door,
Two little white rabbits run out of my shoes;
Two doves fly out of my cardigan.
They move around in my home.

5
In silence,
I speak the best words of my heart.
In darkness,
I see the brightest relationship of my heart.

In the far away,
In the furthest away land, lives the closest person to my
heart.

7

What you are offering me in the darkness;
No sun has given it to the earth,
On the brightest summer day.

8

Lonelineoo introduced mo to tho hands that killed me.
Loneliness introduced me to the love that destroyed me.
Loneliness introduced me to the path that lost me.
Loneliness introduced me:
To the suffering that filled me with patience and sturdiness;
To the pride and dignity of a tree grown on a high mountain.
Loneliness kills me and a mountain hides my death.

9

I am full of myself, full of myself and full of myself,
Stubborn just like death itself.
On this planet that is full of suffering and loneliness,
If my hands and my apples aged, died and dropped off;
Except for himself, I shall not offer them to anyone else.

10

Your love is decisive:
Between being and not being;
Between pleasure and pain;
Between disbelief and religious belief.

11

The land of love
Or heavens
Or Barahut.[36]

12

The space between a queen,
And an unfortunate woman
Is merely a man's throne.
Between the dying,
And the revival of women,
There is merely the hand of a man.
Between death,
And the birth of a woman,
There is only the heart of a man.

13

The forest, to prove autumn is arriving,
Drops all her leaves,
Until the morning, from a cloud
Gives hundreds of speeches.
Jesus, to prove he is the Son of God,
Puts the cross on his shoulders.
To prove that I love you,
I unloaded my apples into a sea
And open the doors myself,
But when my womanhood was crucified
Neither he nor God feel my suffering,
Or are ready to forgive me.

---

36 Barahut is one of the valleys of hell which collects the souls of infidels and hypocrites, according to Islam.

14

The suffering of Farough is in my soul,[37]
Who left me for loneliness, death and torture,
But this is not Tehran.
I am in doubt and confused by complex relationships.
I have been saddened by the suffering of motherhood,
And being near and far away from my son.
Oh my son!
Burning in my own heart;
Burning in my own home;
Burning in my own dignity;
Like the burning of Farough,
But this is not Tehran.

15

In the home of my suffering, I am lonely.
In the journey of uncertain fate, I am lonely.
In the stroll of the gardens
And running within the corridors of hell, I am alone.
A window has not offered me kindness, not even once.
Ever since I was born, the garden has been in one hand, and
I am in the other.

16

I am not proud of you, the darkest species,
And the deadliest relationship.

---

37 Forugh Farrokhzad (January 5th 1935 — February 13th 1967) was a film director
and an influential Iranian female poet. She is an iconic figure who died in a car
accident at the age of 32.

I am detached from the stones on my father's chest.
I am detached from my mother's destroyed looks.
I am detached from a homeland that, as far as she had the
power to fight;
And as long as there was power in despair,
She pushed us away towards the borders.
She pushed us on the roads where our dignity died
And our hearts left beauty forever.
I am not proud of you, naïve suffering.

17
My loneliness and isolation,
Look like him.
My thinking ties me to a person:
Like Jesus is forgiving;
Like Mahdi is non-reaching;[38]

Like flying has no limit.

My beauty, my pride,
My boundless suffering,
The doubts and my shattered heart,
Are invaded by a person,
Who like death, is heartless,
And like love, full of life.

My loneliness,
Hesitation and sadness,
Neither is lost in the truth
Nor would it brighten up in my doubts,
Whether it is on the street;
In the house;
Or in the mosque.

18

A star can
Fill my night with light and the colour of Eros.[39]
The soft hands of sunrays, in the morning,
When they touch the window,
Can brighten up my day,
And run through my vision like a river.

A dark angry cloud,
Despite having you in my heart,
Can narrow the avenues further down;

---

38 Mahdi is the prophesied redeemer of Islam who is believed to rule before the Day of Judgment.

39 In Greek mythology, Eros was the God of Love.

Fill up my heart with such darkness,
That from feeling alienated and disoriented,
I start crying.
As much as I am the slave of the sky;
I enslave my own heart.

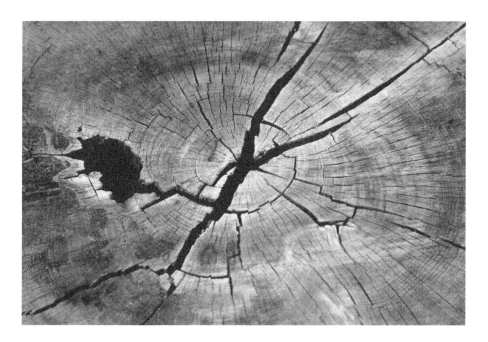

The Sadness Dictionary

Childhood – the period that we have never experienced;
Not even in black and white photographs.

Friends – the loneliness forces us,
To end up in front of their doors.

Homeland – did not offer me a room

In which I could dream;
Did not even give me a dream,
So that I could build a room for her.

The poet – whose pen
Beheaded poems
And hurt so many of us.
More than the sword of the fundamentalist,
When we were queuing to gain our imagination
During a gathering,
There is always a possibility,
That unexpectedly terminates our reassurance.

Beauty – half of it was violated
In the smoke of conflicts,
And the other half was exiled.

The Eastern man – When he experiences
The shy and withdrawn breasts of the fearful East,
He is extremist, conservative and irritated.
When he experiences
Open-eyed, outgoing and freed Western breasts,
He bows to his knees,
He is tolerant, liberal and deeply in love.

BARZAN OSMAN

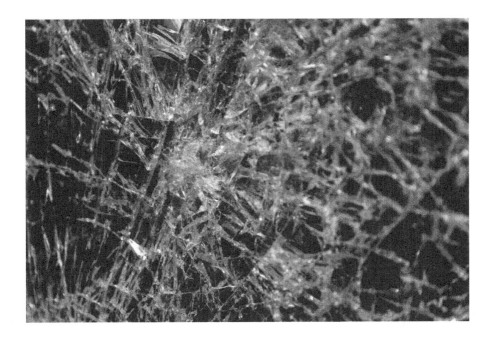

Barzan Osman was more of a theatre professional than a poet. When we were schoolmates in the 1970s, we acted in a play together in the Sulaymaniyah Secondary school theatre. He later joined the Kurdish resistance movement; however, in the early 1980s he was captured by Saddam's security men and was sadly murdered and his corpse was pulled behind a military vehicle in the city of Sulaymaniyah. I have translated one of his very well-known lyrics, which was later set to music and sung by Mohammad Abbas Bahram.

I met Osman in my secondary school. We were in different classes and grew closer whilst both of us were together in a play. We spent considerable time in and outside school. He was on his way to become a successful actor, but death did not give him the chance.

Fire with no Ash

Your golden tresses like a chain tie my hands and legs;
Your burning eyes like an arrow strike the mirror of your
face.

A fire with no ash is my heart that is aflame.
A fire with no ash is my heart that is burning.

Your eyes seem quiet, calm and sad.
But you hide, beneath your glance, coquetry and magic.

It is the same old hidden sly flirtation,
Slowly and calmly crushing the flower of hope.

It is not just mine; you have broken many hearts.
It is this cruel treatment you have inflicted on me.

My heart is burning for you without ashes.
And I have given you my heart; why did you have to stomp
on it?

A fire with no ash is my heart that is aflame.
A fire with no ash is my heart that is burning.

ESMAYIL MOHAMMED

Esmayil Mohammed is a Kurdish poet who lives in Sulaymaniyah, the Kurdistan region of Iraq. From an early age, he had his own recognisable style. The first poem here inspired the title of this anthology. Most of his poetry concentrates on love for women. Mohammed writes in a simple style, recognises with ordinary people.

My Poetry Depicts You

All my poems are a depiction of you; why do you burn your
images?
Show me a single one of them that avoids your reflection!
One of them is fair like your hair; one red rose painting your
lips;
One portrays your eyes, magical and mysterious.
You can burn all my poems; you may never even name me,
But whoever sees you would know, my poetry depicts you.

If You Pay Me a Visit

If you pay me a visit, no need to knock on the door.
Wouldn't I recognise your footsteps!
If you think you cannot be mine,
Instead of a flower, allow my unfortunate soul
To dangle on your tresses.

Women

They say, I love women beyond limits; I say, for being very
kind.
They are a heaven of passion and the springs of poetry.
That is why to my last breath, I compose poetry for them.
Without them, most likely, poetry may not have come to be.

Impossible

I love you; as it is clear to me, you love me too as much;
But neither you nor I can reveal it.

Wouldn't love create the most beautiful world?
Wouldn't love force the impossible on its knees!

You and I

Your letters are packed with sorrows and memories;
When I open them to read, rains of love fall from them.
I don't know what I shall write; how to express my love to
you?
I may as well sacrifice my poetry to you.
My heart is only attracted to you, as if it was created for you.
Till now, no love has matched yours and mine.

Hussein Mawlud Ahmed known as Mala Ali

At midnight on July 22nd 1979, at least three Kurds were hanged by the ousted regime of Saddam Hussein in a prison that specialised in hanging Kurdish prisoners. One of them was Mala Ali, his real name being Hussein Mawlud Ahmed. In accordance with the usual practice of the former regime, his body was not returned to his family. It was instead buried in a graveyard, dedicated entirely to executed prisoners, in Mosul. He was born in 1953 to a simple farming family in a village near the city of Sulaymaniyah.

I met Mala Ali in 1971, when I became the chairman of the Student Union in the Watan Secondary School in Sulaymaniyah. He was also a member. He moved on to higher education before I did. However, we kept in touch to discuss the socio-political issues of the time.

Mala Ali joined *Komelley Ranjderani Kurdistan*, which later became one of the wings of the PUK. He joined the *Peshmerga* forces on May 11th 1977. While he was fighting on a special mission in the Surdash region of Sulaymaniyah, Iraqi Kurdistan, he was ambushed and captured by the Iraqi forces. On June 6th 1979, Mala Ali went on trial in a specific court for Kurds in Kirkuk, and was sentenced to death by hanging.

I never knew Mala Ali as a poet while he was alive. I don't believe he ever wrote poetry before his arrest. He only started writing poetry during his time in prison, from January 30th to July 22nd 1979, and yet he wrote some beautiful poems with a good command of the language. Under Saddam's rule, no literature was allowed to leave the prison, but his sister-in-law, Naza Hassan, the wife of his twin brother, managed to retrieve the poems successfully.

They have become an extremely important part of literature ever since, as not many writings were released from prison under Saddam Hussein's reign. These are rare pieces written by an individual who awaited the noose.

I Wished Not to Die Young

What shall I do! My plan was destroyed by death.
The enemy pours my blood into his wine glass.[40]

Yes, they believe that they'll eliminate me.
Without their knowledge, they take me towards the sun.

Towards the sun, and I shall be ready;
Where I become a ray of light in every home.

Another few days before the gallows;
I'll be taken to die while I am fully conscious.

Even if the enemy became a monster,
Begging will not leave my lips.
The pains of torture, imprisonment, fetter and noose,
Would not bow my head to the enemies.

I shall drink courageously the wine of death.
Who cares, at least my friends are safe!

But when I wished not to die young,
Kurdistan said: I need his efforts.

Love, Faith, Trust and Promise

Love, faith, trust and promise,

---

40 Mala Ali wrote this poem on July 7th 1979, fifteen days before his execution.
He was kept in the Execution quarter in Mosul Prison.

With myself, I bury all of them in a grave.
I have seen too many pass me by as I was waiting;
Thousands of wishes will die with me.

I have lost poetry, photos and memories;
They all ended up like myself in the hands of life.

What is left behind after my death,
Are a few cassettes of recorded songs.

Mamle, Sharokh, Zirak and Dilan,[41]
Now, listening to them is prohibited to inmates.
I am faithful to them, even in prison.
I wish them to be handed down to Ahmad after my death.[42]

To the Gallows

My brother is far away and so are my relatives.
The age immaturely takes me higher.
It is certain that my walk leads me to the gallows.
The red flag wears my blood like henna on feet.
Towards the room, towards the room of the gallows,
Has exhausted me, yet my place is damp.
While the signs of distress appear on me;
They are wounds of torture and marks of beating.

Do not say, he dies and is fearful of death; he is stressed.
If I am a *Peshmerga*; I will always be ahead of you.

---

[41] They are Kurdish singers.

[42] Ahmed is the poet's twin brother, who passed away a few years after the execution of Mala Ali.

I am glad for a death that is before yours.
My face always wears the smile of happiness.

Despite that, I am on my way to the last home of life.
The first home of eternity is visible from here.
Because my fate won't be a death in bed;
I am happy for being on my feet to my very last breath.

I wouldn't exchange such a death with many lives.
A life that offers my head to the enemy as a fence.
It is a pride that I see my shoes,
Over the head of my enemies when I rise.

I step on them and look;
Towards the town of my resting caravan.
I catch up with others whose footprints are visible.
Here and as far as I can, I shall follow them.

Now I follow a frontrunner,
Who was here, before me, a few nights ago.
It is clear that I stayed as long as he did.
I am going to take a short nap in his bed.

I cover myself with a blanket left from him;
To ease out the pains of my ailing body.
It is evident that I am following in his steps;
Who knows who else will put his feet in my divine place.

Yet again, I have another road ahead of me;
The road to the graveyard, where I'm sure he will be
present.
If it is not decent for my body to replace his,

Then my soul will be a butterfly amongst the flowers of his grave.

Which will be regarded as a pride;
And I am ready to play with my life in this way.
While his blood is offered in this struggle;
My blood will also help to paint his path.

The death that is fearful of me, I shall comfort.
Why doesn't it come to put me down!
Let it get to know me: I am a *Peshmerga* of *Komala;*[43]
And a cedar who has a clean hand and a clean past.

When after death there is a new world,
By that time, let my soul sleep very well.
Because the resurrection day creates an opportunity,
To take another duty like the one I have already.

In that world, I shall still be a *Peshmerga* and cedar;
At least I shall be better than what I am now.
Here, I have experiences of the struggle path;
There, I shall be fire in the revolution furnace.

If I am not able to fight here;
There, my weapon is in the hands of one of my friends.
If I am left behind from the caravan here;
There, I shall be an elite in front of the convoy.

---

[43] Komala is one of the political groups that formed the PUK.

BAKIR ALI

Bakir Ali (June 16th 1968 – September 1st 1994) was not given an opportunity to live long, although his poetic talent was obvious from an early age. Before his unfortunate death, he was well-known among his generation. He mostly lived in the city of Sulaymaniyah.

Coming from a deprived background, he was politically active and became the voice of his class of people. Ali was one of the leaders of a peaceful protest on September 1st 1994, when he was shot dead allegedly by Kurdish security forces. Ali was not deemed a threat, as he was a peaceful protester. Fourteen days before his death, Ali was arrested by the Kurdistan security forces and was released six days later.

People close to Ali confirmed that he was gravely tortured. Below is an account of the events that led to Ali's death, on September 1st 1994. The protest was over a shanty town in a quarter of Sulaymaniyah, where underprivileged people built their properties after the collapse of Saddam Hussein's regime in several parts of Kurdistan in 1991. The Kurdish authorities, established in the security vacuum left by the withdrawal of the Baghdad regime, announced that the properties were illegal and must be evacuated, without providing any alternative for the vast population living there. Ali's family had occupied one of these properties. He was one of the organisers of the protest which led to his detainment by the security forces prior to the protest taking place.

On the day of the protest, September 1st 1994, the population of the shanty town gathered in front of the governor's building. The authorities used live ammunitions to scatter people. People were driven into chaos and fearing for their lives they ran away in different directions. Ali had started to run away. However, some security forces, whose names are known, followed him and shot him from the back. He fell, wounded. To ensure that he was dead, Ali was shot in the mouth. I suspect it was a symbolic act to keep him quiet and set example for others. The security man who shot Ali was later killed during the Kurdish internal conflict between the Patriotic Union of Kurdistan (PUK), led by late Jalal Talabani, and the Kurdistan Democratic Party (KDP) led by Masoud Barzani.

In 1993, he self-published a modest collection of his poetry, only 34 pages, entitled, *Those nights are darker than your tresses*. In 2010, the first edition of his poetry was published on the anniversary of his death. In 2015, Ghazalnus Publishing House published the second edition. The Kurdistan authorities refused to provide the publishing house with a registration number, a local number similar to an ISBN required to be obtained from the authorities, reporting that the book contained defamation. Despite this, the publishing house went ahead and no legal action was taken against them.

Sadly, his death was never investigated and subsequently caused people to mistrust the Kurdistan administration. Ironically two of Ali's brothers were executed in the Abu-Ghreb Prison in 1989 by Saddam Hussein's regime, because they were accused of their association with the PUK; and yet Ali was killed by PUK authorities in Sulaymaniyah.

Borders

I am leaving,
Please tell her
She will not see me again.

I am leaving,
And when I leave, like streams of water,
I shall not turn back.

I am tired of where I am,
Of the trees and the stones.
I am tired of her town, herself,
Her mirror, hair clips and combs.
I am tired of her tresses,
Of her domesticated hands and fingers.

I loved you and I thought

From the day I loved you,
You were a sad butterfly
Landing on my eyelashes.
I loved you; I thought
You were as clear as my tears.

I thought, if I were Lake Zrebar,[44]
You would still be deeper than my soul.

Alas,
Oh my Iranian gazelle,
Oh clean prayers of my poetry,
I am no match for your love.

You said, you wished to visit me.
Please don't arrive here!
This land would not allow you
To be married to one of my poems;
I am leaving.

Alas, here,
In the Iran of Jibba, Turban and black magic,
In every military barrack,
In every army base, and
At every checkpoint,
My briefcase has to be checked.
So how could I
Bring some single hairs of the gazelle's tresses,
To my homeland?

---

44 Zrebar is a lake in the Meriwan district in Kurdistan – Iran.

IRFAN AHMAD

Irfan Ahmed (August 31st 1963 – August 5th 2012) died in his birthplace of Sulaymaniyah. It is believed that his poem "Mother, you are leaving!", which became a well-known Kurdish song, is what made Ahmed become widely known amongst Kurds. Other Kurdish artists also included verses of his poem in their songs.

Unfortunately, he was never given the chance to write as a more mature adult. On July 31st 2012, the Kurdish security forces in Sulaymaniyah detained Ahmed for reasons that still remain unknown. On August 1st 2012, he was hospitalised, but his family was only informed the following day. When they went to visit him in the hospital, he was in a coma. The doctors demonstrated to them the extent of the beatings given to him; he suffered all over his body including a 10-cm cut on his head. He later died in the hospital on August 5th 2012. Sadly, he never regained consciousness to tell his story and the authorities never investigated his death. He left behind his wife and daughter.

You don't sleep!

You don't sleep, and the moon is as bright as the flame of a candle;
You don't sleep, and the dark night is waiting for a moment of sunrise.

I have made your pillow out of yellow autumn leaves;
I have woven your curtain out of silks of love;
And yet you don't sleep.

I tell you about phonograms to feel the taste;
I tell you about bunnies who jump over their fears.

I tell you about boats, the wind blowing their canvasses;
To throw their fate onto the waves.

You don't sleep!
The night is reaching up to my knees;
And my glass reveals I am tipsy;
You burned half of my intensity;
I burned half of my liveliness.

I have made your pillow out of yellow autumn leaves;
I have knitted your curtain out of silks of love;
And yet you don't sleep.

Early tomorrow,
We will draw the scattered fringes of the sunray over the
window,
To wipe its wet forehead.

Early tomorrow,
We will frame the cloud;
And nail it with four drops of rain.
Later we'll visit a bazaar to buy
A handful of love.

Early tomorrow,
But you have to sleep now.

INSPIRED

The poems in this section are not direct translations; rather inspired by poets who influenced me.

Life Restlessly Passes Away

Inspired by a number of Sufi poets

The location of the heart cannot be reached by
Streams of love.
When I am doomed,
Love is nowhere and can't rescue me.

Day follows night, night follows day.
Life restlessly passes away
Cutting deeply into my entity;
And yet I still fight the shadow
Over my path,
With an old sword left long ago
With my long gone ancestors.

At night, I put my head on the pillow,
All alone.
I close my eyes, and as I am about to sleep,
I stay awake to the next day.
No beauty comes to kiss me,
Putting her head over my heart
And saying,
Don't you worry!
I will stay,
I will even be here to the day
When your soul has to depart.

Wineglass

Inspired by Omar Khayyam 45

I witness the sunrise, I kiss the dawn.
The day does not stay,
I anxiously wait for the sunset.

At dusk, every day,

---

45 Omar Khayyam (May 18th, 1048 – December 4th 1131) – Persian polymath,
scholar, mathematician, astronomer, philosopher and poet.

I cannot pour myself a glass,
Unless I bow,
To my wineglass - made of clay.
Once almost full,
Then, she would not allow me
To have my sips,
Unless I raise her high in respect,
And kiss her on the lips.
I do not mind;
As in the past, even this little pot,
Was once a heartbreaking beauty,
Who had not yet lost her pride.

When it breaks, the wine glass
Mixes up with the earth,
Turns back to clay,
But not before everyone,
Royalties and commoners,
Bowing to her
And kissing her day after day.
The more they drank,
The lower they bowed,
And the more kisses she received,
Year after year.

When she dies,
She will shatter to announce her passing away.
As for myself,
In total silence, I take my share,
To turn back into clay,
Just like her.

Time to Depart

Inspired by Bekhud[46]

In the gloom of the night,
I lost my shadow.
On the foggy narrow path,
I lost my vision.
When I look around,
My loved ones have all vanished.
I am the one left behind
In this barren land,
I am left with no choice
Except to carry the sorrow of the whole.
And then my heart tells my soul,
It is time for you to depart.

Life and Death

Inspired by Mansur al-Hallaj[47]

With my death, my life flourishes,
Though death is hidden in my life,
And life is hidden in my death.
My birth occurs only once,
My death is with me every day

I am the Truth, keeping life and death apart.

---

[46] Inspired by Bekhud (1879 – 1955) or Mullah Mahmud Mufti, Kurdish poet, social and religious leader.

[47] Inspired by Mansur al-Hallaj (March 26th 858 - March 26th 922) - Sufi mystic, poet and leading Sufi thinker.

I am the sun, to separate day and night.
And a night, long and dark
Leading dusk to dawn;
You may burn me,
With the bones buried deeply in graveyards,
My soul may depart, but I stay as the Eternal Truth.

Tomorrow After Dawn

Tomorrow, just after dawn,
I visit the garden of God,
Near paradise.
I pick one thousand and one fresh roses.
Then, I climb the highest mountain peak,
Close to God,
To reach out to rays of sacred sunlight.
I weave the rays like my mother's braid,
To wrap my picked roses
And make a bouquet of flowers.

After a rest,
Late under the moonlight,
With my soul,
When the moon and darkness fight,
On every petal of each rose,
I tell one of my beautiful love stories,
Hidden deeply
Inside my heart.
With a handwriting,
As neat as my brother's death;
So that for one thousand and one night,

In peace,
You embrace your sleep.

Departing

For your next trip,
I want you to travel light.

Before you depart,
Leave all your tender love behind,
For me.
I'll keep it safe in my heart.

Only take away
Our sweet memories
With you,
So that we are never apart.

Lips

I drank a glass of love through your red lips.
In the secret of your vivid eyes,
I hover like a bird,
To be born again without sins.
I am tipsy with the wine of your love.
My body started Sufi whirling.
I have no more fear
Of the chief punishment from the Almighty.

Before Knowing You

Before knowing you,
I was always short of time.
The years were months.
The months were weeks.
The weeks were days.
The days were hours.
The hours were minutes.
The minutes were seconds.
I was always short of time.

Now, after knowing you, there is only one time,
Time to meet you.
And this is so far away.
The seconds are minutes.
The minutes are hours.
The hours are days.
The days are weeks.
The weeks are months.
The months are years.

Waiting for you is as long as a lifetime.

Miscellaneous

Nima Youshij

Nima Youshij (November 12th 1896 – January 6th 1960) was an Iranian poet who was well-known for modernising Iranian poetry. His school of poetry was named after him, i.e. *Nimayy.* Youshij. Together with other Iranian poets, he has influenced parts of Kurdish poetry. The following poem "Late at night" is an example of his work.[48]

---

[48] Translated from Farsi to Kurdish, by Nasir Husami

Late at night

Late at night,
During the moment
When shadows seep
Between the branches of the trees,

The love of your sweetheart
Is sad for the darkness of the night.
During that moment
My eyes are watching the road
For you.

Late at night,
During the moment
When the motionless valleys and hills
Are the body of a soulless serpent.

During that moment
When the convolvulus, like a lover,
Embraces the bodies of the pine trees,
Whether I am in your memory or not
My mind is only with you.
In the way that I came to being,
My eyes are still watching the road
For you.

Baba Taher Hamadani

International mystic, saint and poet Baba Taher Hamadani
(1000-1060) lived in Hamadan, today's Iran.

1

I count stars, as the night comes;
An endless fight, a far too long wait.
If you don't arrive just at midnight,
I bring clouds, thunder and storm.

2

The life has passed slowly, you didn't come
During the scent of springtime, you didn't come
I said: I only wish to see you to inform you:
Being without you is unbearable, you didn't come.

3

The cool night, lush surrounding, and such a moonlight
Let us drink; there may not be another chance
The moon shines, spring will come back, it is only us,
Who die and become green and soil here and there.

Hamdi

Hamdi or Ahmed Bag Fatah Bag (1876 - 1936), was a Kurdish classical poet who lived in Sulaymaniyah.

Dawns do not smile, unless destitution cries over night;
Flowers do not bloom, unless the morning nightingale cries
deeply from her heart;
The trees in the world's garden do not yell fruits, unless we
all together,
With one voice, with one emotion and with one tear, cry over
each branch.

Mahwi

Mahwi, (aka: Mala Mohammed Osman Ballkhi) (1830-1906)
Kurdish Sufi, thinker and classical poet.

What shall I do? I am not the soul that helps one to be a
soul;
Nor I have reached the soul that makes me a soul.

If it is the result of your soul that no soul is left around you.
Give up your soul, and do not take refuge in a soul!

Being Far away or close

Dunya Goran – a Kurdish young lady living in Kurdistan

It is a path full of wonders;
I am neither far away from you,
Nor have you lost me.
All I know,
I am so close to you;
I see you lost and inexistent.
You went astray in the eyes of the musicians.
Your sweet voice is vanished;
Not signing happy songs anymore.
I am so close to you,
I see,
The streets of the town
Turn their lights on;
And walk closer,
To be inspired by you.

Biography

Dr Rebwar Fatah moved to live in exile in London in 1982. He

 extensively contributes towards the understanding of Middle Eastern issues. He has written numerous articles, given talks and interviews, in both Kurdish and English, on the socio-political situation of the Middle East. He works as a Middle Eastern expert and speaks the main languages thereof fluently. Dr Rebwar Fatah holds BSc, MSc and PhD degrees from the University of London and the University College London (UCL).

As a young man and throughout his life, Dr Fatah has written and translated poetry with a passion for language, peace, acknowledgement and free expression.

Dr Fatah is the author of Hawkar – The Newsletter of Hawkarani Kurdistan, available from Amazon.